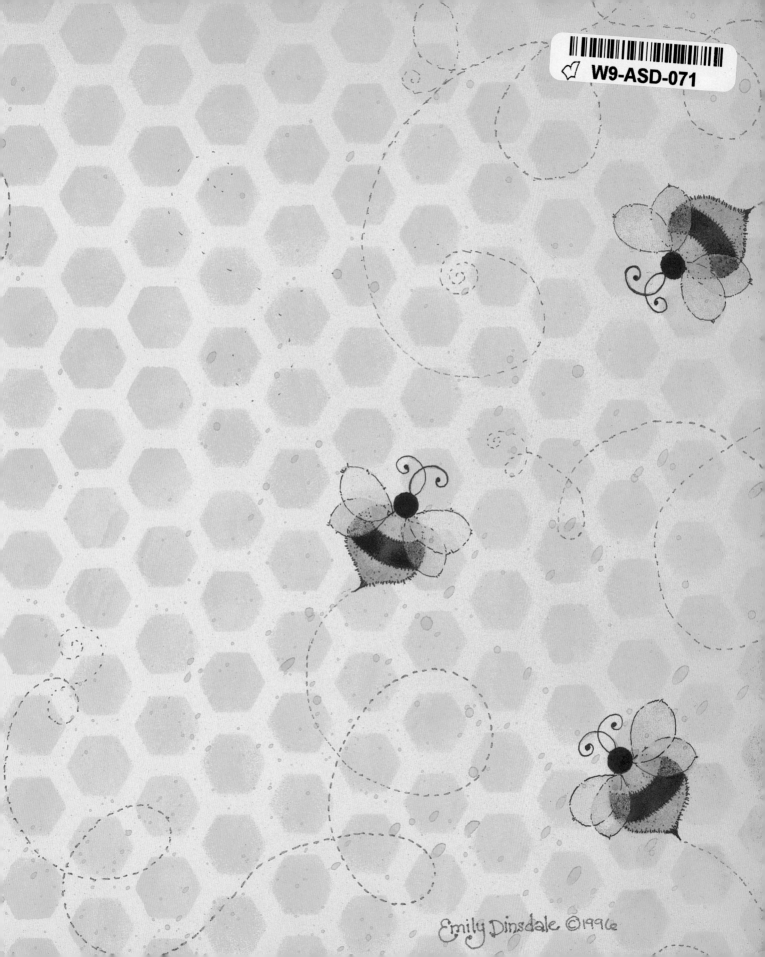

Emily Dinsdale ©1996

DECORATIVE PAINTED WOOD PROJECTS

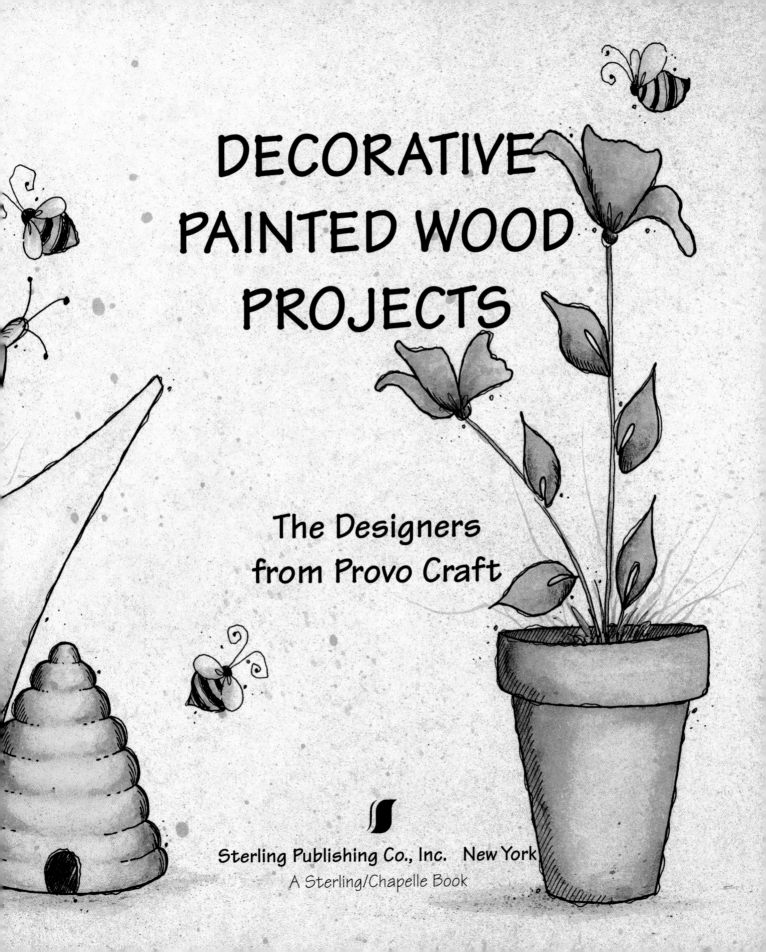

DECORATIVE PAINTED WOOD PROJECTS

The Designers from Provo Craft

Sterling Publishing Co., Inc.   New York

A Sterling/Chapelle Book

FOR CHAPELLE:

Owner: Jo Packham

Editor: Cathy Sexton

Staff: Malissa Boatwright, Kass Burchett, Rebecca Christensen, Shirley Heslop, Holly Hollingsworth,
    Susan Jorgensen, Susan Laws, Amanda McPeck, Barbara Milburn, Pat Pearson, Leslie Ridenour,
    Cindy Rooks, and Cindy Stoeckl

Designers: Rebecca Carter, Emily Dinsdale, Kathy Distefano Griffiths, Debbie Crabtree Lewis, and Jill Webster

Photographer: Kevin Dilley / Hazen Photography • Photo Stylists: Jo Packham, Susan Laws, and Cindy Rooks

If you have any questions or comments or would like information on specialty products featured in this book, please contact Chapelle, Ltd., Inc., P.O. Box 9252, Ogden, UT 84409 • (801) 621-2777 • (801) 621-2788 Fax

Library of Congress Cataloging-in-Publication Data

Decorative painted wood projects / the designers from Provo Craft.
        p.   cm.
    "A Sterling / Chapelle book."
    Includes index.
    ISBN 0-8069-8141-5
     1. Woodwork--Patterns. 2. Painting. 3. Painted woodwork.
    4. Wood finishing. I. Provo Craft (Group).
    TT200.D43   1997
    745.7'23--dc20   96-24640
                                                                  CIP

10 9 8 7 6 5 4 3 2 1

Published by Sterling Publishing Company, Inc.
387 Park Avenue South, New York, NY 10016
© 1996 by Chapelle Ltd.
Distributed in Canada by Sterling Publishing
c/o Canadian Manda Group, One Atlantic Avenue, Suite 105
Toronto, Ontario, Canada M6K 3E7
Distributed in Great Britain and Europe by Cassell PLC
Wellington House, 125 Strand, London WC2R 0BB, England
Distributed in Australia by Capricorn Link (Australia) Pty Ltd.
P.O. Box 6651, Baulkham Hills, Business Centre, NSW 2153, Australia
Printed in Hong Kong
All Rights Reserved

Sterling ISBN 0-8069-8141-5

Contents

General Instructions 6

Assembling Windmills & Whirligigs 9

Plaid Chicken Boxes 10

Sitting Rabbit Garden Stake 14

Sitting Rooster Garden Stake 17

Old Mac's Farm 20

Guardian Bunny 24

Country Girl 28

Welcome Bee Keeper 32

Cock-A-Doodle-Doo Chalkboard 42

Barnyard Friends Chalkboard 45

Ladybug Windmill 48

Honey Bear Windmill 52

Cat & Bird Windmill 55

Beehive Whirligig 58

Watering Can Whirligig 59

Rabbit on Rooster Whirligig 62

Noah & Friends Whirligig 65

Bunny & Carrots Whirligig 70

Fat Cat Wind Chime 73

Ark Wind Chime 76

Every Bunny Loves A Garden Wind Chime 81

Rooster Weathervane 84

Dove Weathervane 87

S.S. Ark Weathervane 90

To The Garden Sign 94

Birdhouse Welcome 98

Birdhouse with Dormers 101

3-Hole Birdhouse & Cat 104

Birdhouse For Rent 108

Pine Shingles Birdhouse 112

Rosebud Birdhouse 117

Birdhouse Planter Box 120

Picket Fence Planter 124

Metric Conversion Chart 127

Index 128

General Instructions

Preparing Wood for Painting:

Supplies needed:
- Photocopy machine
- Transfer paper
- Pencil or stylus
- Kneaded eraser
- Band saw or scroll saw
- Sandpaper,
    medium- & fine-grit
- Tack cloth
- Water- or oil-base sealer

Begin by transferring the pattern(s) onto the wood to be used for a specific project. First, make a photocopy of the original patterns found in this book. Make sure to enlarge those where enlargements are necessary. Slip a piece of transfer paper, transfer side down, between the photocopy and the wood to be used. Using a pencil or a stylus, trace the outline(s) of the shape(s) to be cut from the wood. Using an appropriate saw, cut out the shape(s).

Sand the cut-outs to create a smooth painting surface. Some woods may need to be sanded before sealing. Whenever possible, sand wood in the direction of the grain. Check to make sure all flat surfaces and all edges are smooth to the touch. Remove the dust with a tack cloth.

Sealing the wood helps prevent the wood grain from raising. Water-base sealers usually dry in about 15 minutes. Oil-base sealers usually dry in about seven hours, but it is recommended to let oil-base sealed wood dry overnight.

When wood sealer is thoroughly dry, lightly sand wood and remove the dust with a tack cloth. Transfer all details and essential lines from the photocopy of the original pattern onto the sealed wood using the same method as previously described. When transferring, use very light pressure to avoid heavy lines. If necessary, unwanted lines can be removed with a kneaded eraser.

When it is necessary to transfer pattern details onto surfaces that have already been painted, use graphite paper on light-colored areas and white graphite paper on dark-colored areas.

Adding Dots:

When adding dots, always use fresh acrylic paint. Hold the "dotter" (pointed end of a paintbrush, stylus, or corsage pin) in a vertical position and dip it into the fresh paint. Put it down on the surface and pull it straight up. When the dots need to be consistent in size, re-load the dotter each time. For descending dots, dip the dotter in the paint once, then continue adding dots until the paint runs out. Cleaning the dotter between dots will assure the dots remain round.

Antique Finishing:

A vintage look can be imitated by using an antique spray stain. Simply spray the outer edges of the project. Short bursts of spray will spatter the project and give a nice soft look.

Allow the spray stain to dry thoroughly and finish with a spray varnish.

Antiquing:

To antique wood surfaces, use an antiquing medium. Apply the antiquing medium by rubbing it over wood surfaces with a clean cloth, wiping off any excess. Allow the antiquing medium to dry thoroughly. Repeat the process for a richer, darker color. Antiquing medium can also be used as a stain.

Base Coating (Painting):

Apply acrylic paint to all painting surfaces for full, opaque coverage. Cover the area with two to three smooth, even coats of paint. It is better to apply several thin coats of paint, rather than one heavy coat. Allow paint to dry thoroughly between coats. When the paint causes the wood grain to raise, lightly sand painted surfaces before applying additional coats. When painting the fronts and the backs of any wood shape, the edges should also be painted.

When painting on chalkboard slates, the first coat of paint may bead up because of its slick surface. Do not worry. Simply apply a second coat for complete coverage.

Curling Wire:

Curl wire by wrapping it around a pencil, a wooden dowel, or a paintbrush handle. After wrapping, pull the object used out of the coil and repeat the process if the coil needs to be longer than the length of the object being used.

Dry Brushing:

Load a round fabric dye brush with a small amount of acrylic paint. Wipe the brush on a paper towel until there is very little paint left. Hold the brush in a vertical position and apply the paint using a circular motion moving from the center to the outside. The color will soften toward the outer edges.

Float Shading:

This technique is used to apply shading and highlighting. Dampen the largest flat brush that will accommodate the area to be float-shaded. Wipe the brush on a paper towel until there is very little water left. Load one corner of the brush, up to $1/3$ of the width of the chisel edge, with acrylic paint. Stroke the brush back and forth on a palette to work the paint into the bristles and soften the color. Apply the brush to the painting surface. The paint color should appear darkest at the loaded corner and gradually fade to clear water on the opposite corner. If the paint spreads all the way across the chisel edge of the bristles, rinse the brush and re-load.

Linework:

Outline a project, or areas within a project, with a liner brush and acrylic paint or with permanent markers. The size of the tip on the marker may vary depending on the effect desired. Various colored paints or inks can be used. When using permanent markers, a matte spray varnish must be used for sealing the artwork. Other types of varnish will cause the ink to run.

7

Spattering:

Wet an old toothbrush and shake or blot off excess water. Dip the bristles of the toothbrush into acrylic paint that has been slightly diluted with water. Hold the toothbrush about 6 to 8 inches away with the bristles pointed toward the project. Draw a finger or thumb across the bristles toward you causing the paint to spatter onto the painted project. The size of the spatters depends on the amount of water used to dilute the paint — using more water results in larger spatters; less water results in smaller spatters.

Stenciling:

This technique is used to force paint through a pre-cut surface. Apply the chosen stencil to the project — either hold it or tape it securely. Stenciling adhesive is also available and can be used. Load a stencil or round fabric dye brush with a small amount of acrylic paint or stenciling cream. Wipe the brush on a paper towel to remove excess paint (or cream). Stipple the paint into the open areas of the stencil. Too much paint on the brush will cause the paint to seep under the stencil. It is better to use less paint and apply several coats.

Stippling:

This technique is simply a way to apply acrylic paint by repeated small touches. Flat brushes, stencil brushes, round fabric dye brushes, or cosmetic sponges — new or worn out — can be used. Load the brush with paint and wipe it on a paper towel to remove excess paint. Hold the brush in a vertical position and pounce the brush up and down to apply the paint. The more paint in the brush, the more solid the effect. Less paint in the brush produces a soft, light effect. It is better to use less paint and apply several coats. Allow paint to dry thoroughly between coats.

Stroking:

Stroke acrylic paint in by taking the tip of a brush and, using pressure, pulling it toward you. Slowly release the pressure until you get a point.

Varnishing:

A coat of spray varnish, applied to the finished painted project, will help protect it. Use an acrylic-based spray varnish in either a matte- or gloss-finish. Water-based varnishes are also available and can be used but, like gloss-finish spray varnishes, they will cause the ink to run if linework has been done with a permanent marker.

Washing:

This technique refers to the application of acrylic paint to a surface for transparent coverage. Mix the paint with water in a 1:3 ratio (25% paint to 75% water). Apply this paint wash to sealed wood. Several coats of a light wash produce a soft, but deep, transparent color. Allow wash to dry thoroughly between coats. When the wash causes the wood grain to raise, lightly sand washed surfaces before applying additional coats.

Assembling Windmills & Whirligigs

Windmills:

Supplies needed for small windmills:
Wooden dowel: (1) $^3/_8$" diameter x 1" length
Wooden hub: (1) 1" diameter x $^3/_8$" thick
Round-head wood screw: (1) #4 x 1"

Before assembling windmills, the wooden dowel and wooden hub should be painted or stained according to the project instructions. The round-head wood screw should not be painted.

Drill one $^3/_{32}$" hole in one end of the wooden dowel. Drill one $^1/_8$" hole in the center of the wooden hub. Cut four $^1/_4$" deep grooves, $^1/_8$" wide around the wooden hub. The grooves must be cut at 45° angles.

To assemble, glue the wooden dowel inside the drilled hole in the project piece with wood glue. Make sure the drilled end is exposed. Insert the wood screw through the drilled hole in the center of the wooden hub and screw the wooden hub to the wooden dowel. Do not tighten — it must turn easily. Glue the windmill pieces into the angled grooves.

Whirligigs:

Supplies needed for small whirligigs:
Wooden dowels:
(1) $^5/_{16}$" diameter x 1$^1/_2$" length
(2) $^5/_{16}$" diameter x 1" length
Round-head wood screws: (2) #2 x $^5/_8$"

Supplies needed for medium whirligigs:
Wooden dowels:
(1) $^3/_8$" diameter x 2" length
(2) $^3/_8$" diameter x 1$^1/_8$" length
Round-head wood screws: (2) #4 x 1"
Washers: (2) $^3/_{16}$"

Supplies needed for large whirligigs:
Wooden dowels:
(1) $^3/_4$" diameter x 3$^1/_4$" length
(2) $^3/_4$" diameter x 2$^3/_4$" length
Round-head wood screws: (2) #7 x 1$^1/_2$"
Washers: (4) $^3/_{16}$"

Before assembling whirligigs, the wooden dowels should be painted or stained according to the project instructions. The round-head wood screws and washers should not be painted.

For small whirligigs, drill one $^1/_{16}$" hole in each end of the longest wooden dowel. Drill one $^3/_{32}$" hole through the middle of both remaining wooden dowels. Cut $^3/_{16}$" deep grooves, $^1/_8$" wide in each end of these two wooden dowels. The grooves must be cut opposite each other.

For medium whirligigs, drill one $^5/_{64}$" hole in each end of the longest wooden dowel. Drill one $^1/_8$" hole through the middle of both remaining wooden dowels. Cut $^3/_8$" deep grooves, $^1/_8$" wide in each end of these two wooden dowels. The grooves must be cut opposite each other.

For large whirligigs, drill one $^1/_8$" hole in each end of the longest wooden dowel. Drill one $^{11}/_{64}$" hole through the middle of both remaining wooden dowels. Cut $^3/_4$" deep grooves, $^1/_8$" wide in each end of these two wooden dowels. The grooves must be cut opposite each other.

To assemble, insert the longest dowel through the drilled hole in the project piece. Insert the wood screws through the drilled holes in the middle of the two wooden dowels. When using washers, place them between the wood screws and the wooden dowels and between the wooden dowels and the wooden dowel that goes through the piece. Screw each wooden dowel to the wooden dowel that goes through the piece. Do not tighten — it must turn easily. Glue the whirligig paddles into the grooves. Place a small amount of wood glue into drilled hole in piece to secure whirligig assembly.

9

Plaid Chicken Boxes

Designed by Rebecca Carter

Brushes:
Round fabric dye brush: #8
Flat brushes: #2, #4, #8, #12
Liner brush: #2

Acrylic Paint Colors:
Antique white, burnt orange, charcoal grey, cream, evergreen, honey brown, khaki tan, light avocado, light green, midnight blue, red, and true ochre

Supplies:
Papier-mâché boxes:
(1) 4" square x 12" high
(1) 5" square x 13½" high
Cardstock: 2½" wide x 8½" high
Stencils:
⅜" checks & ½" checks
Cellophane tape: ¾"-wide
Permanent black marker, fine-point
Antique spray stain, golden oak
Matte spray varnish
Pinking shears

Small Box:

1. Refer to General Instructions on pages 6-8 for detailed information on painting techniques that are used for this project.

2. Add a decorative border around cardstock with pinking shears.

3. Khaki tan: Paint a 9" x 3" area in the center of each side of box. (Optional: Paint only one side of box with chicken design.)

4. After paint is dry, center cardstock over khaki tan area and hold tightly in place while stippling to make the patch design.

5. Antique white: Stipple around edge of cardstock using a #8 round fabric dye brush. Paint remaining edge with flat brush. (If only one side of box is being painted with chicken design, paint remaining sides of box with antique white.)

6. Burnt orange: Paint orange sections on watermelons.

7. Light green: Paint watermelon rinds.

8. True ochre: Paint sunflowers.

9. Charcoal grey: Paint sunflower centers using a #2 liner brush.

10. Cream: Paint egg and wash stripes on sunflower centers.

11. Red: Paint chicken and watermelon seeds.

12. Burnt orange: Wash wide stripes on chicken. Paint chicken's wattle and comb.

13. Light avocado: Paint box lid, sunflower stems and leaves, and chicken's beak, legs, and feet.

14. Mask off every other row on ⅜" stencil with ¾"-wide cellophane tape that has been cut in half lengthwise.

15. Midnight blue: Stencil $^3/_8$" checks on box lid. Wash wide stripes on box lid and narrow stripes on chicken. Float-shade around chicken's head. Remove tape.

16. Burnt orange: Wash narrow stripes on box lid.

17. Apply eyes and holes on beak with fine-point permanent black marker.

18. Finish with matte spray varnish because of linework.

19. Spray outer edges with antique spray stain.

20. Spray with matte spray varnish again.

Large Box:

1. Refer to General Instructions on pages 6-8 for detailed information on painting techniques that are used for this project.

2. Antique white: Paint border around box bottom.

3. Khaki tan: Paint narrow border on top of antique white border.

4. Evergreen: Paint checks on khaki tan border.

5. Honey brown: Paint remaining box surface.

6. Red: Paint box lid.

7. Light green: Wash wide stripes on box. Paint watermelon rinds on border.

8. Midnight blue: Wash narrow stripes on box.

9. Burnt orange: Stencil $^1/_2$" checks on box lid. Wash wide stripes on box lid. Paint orange sections on watermelons. Paint chicken's beak, legs, and feet.

10. True ochre: Paint sunflowers.

11. Light avocado: Paint sunflower stems and leaves.

12. Red: Paint watermelon seeds and chicken's wattle and comb.

13. Charcoal grey: Paint chicken. Paint sunflower centers using a #2 liner brush.

14. Antique white: Apply dots on chicken and wash stripes on sunflower centers.

15. Midnight blue: Wash narrow stripes on box lid.

16. Line around chicken with fine-point permanent black marker.

17. Finish with matte spray varnish because of linework.

18. Spray outer edges with antique spray stain.

19. Spray with matte spray varnish again.

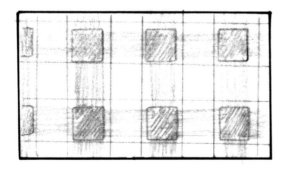

Large Plaid Chicken Box Lid
- Reproduce at 100%
- Paint all four sides

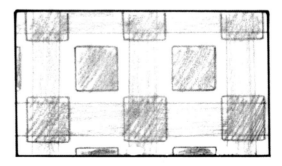

Small Plaid Chicken Box Lid
- Reproduce at 100%
- Paint all four sides

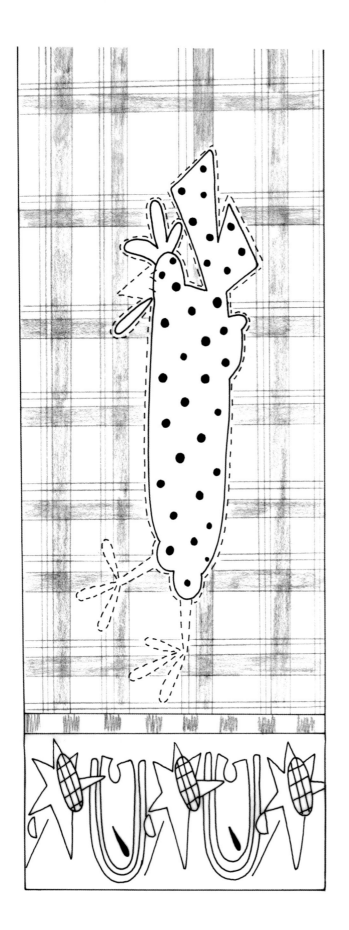

Plaid Chicken Boxes
- Enlarge 150%
- Paint all four sides on each box

Sitting Rabbit Garden Stake

Brushes:
Round fabric dye brushes: #6, #8
Flat brushes: #2, #16
Liner brush: #00
Old toothbrush

Acrylic Paint Colors:
Antique white, black, chocolate, coral, mink, and snow white

Supplies:
Pine for rabbit's body:
   12$\frac{1}{2}$" wide x 12" high x $\frac{3}{4}$" thick
Pine for rabbit's legs:
   14" wide x 5$\frac{1}{2}$" high x $\frac{3}{4}$" thick
Wooden dowel:
   (1) $\frac{1}{2}$" diameter x 12" length
Raffia
Permanent black marker,
   fine-point
Wood glue
Antique spray stain, golden oak
Matte spray varnish
Drill with $\frac{1}{2}$" drill bit

1. Transfer patterns, cut out shapes, and sand and seal wood for painting. Refer to General Instructions on page 6 for a list of supplies needed and for detailed information on preparing wood for painting.

2. Refer to General Instructions on pages 6-8 for detailed information on painting techniques that are used for this project.

3. Paint both sides of rabbit's body identically. Paint only one side of rabbit's legs.

4. Antique white: Paint rabbit's body, rabbit's legs, and wooden dowel.

5. Snow white: Stipple eye areas, tips of ears, center of tail, muzzle, and chest.

6. Coral: Stipple rabbit's cheeks and lower ear openings.

7. Mink: Very lightly stipple rabbit's back, including area where the back meets the tail. Spatter rabbit and rabbit's legs.

8. Chocolate: Paint centers of rabbit's eyes and spatter rabbit.

9. Black: Paint the pupils of the eyes and the points on each side of the eyes.

10. Snow white: Apply dots in eyes.

11. Line rabbit's ears and eyes with fine-point permanent black marker.

12. Lightly spray outer edges with antique spray stain, spraying the front foot and the upper back a little heavier.

13. Using wood glue, glue rabbit's legs to rabbit as shown in photograph on page 14.

14. Finish with matte spray varnish because of linework.

15. Tie a raffia bow around rabbit's neck.

16. Drill one $\frac{1}{2}$" hole in bottom of rabbit for place-ment of wooden dowel.

**Designed by
Debbie
Crabtree Lewis**

17. Using wood glue, glue wooden dowel inside hole in bottom of rabbit. Allow glue to dry thoroughly. Photograph does not show wooden dowel.

Rabbit's Body &
Rabbit's Legs
- Enlarge 150%
- Cut 1 Rabbit
- Cut 2 Legs
- Paint front & back of rabbit's body
- Paint only one side of rabbit's legs

Sitting Rooster Garden Stake

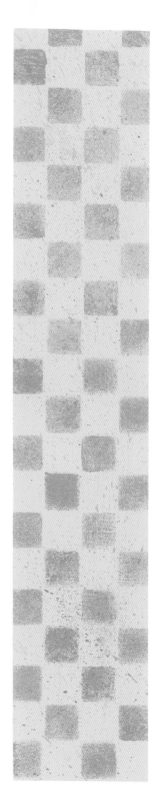

Sitting Rooster Garden Stake

Brushes:
Round fabric dye brushes: #6, #8
Flat brushes: #6, #16
Liner brush: #00
Old toothbrush

Acrylic Paint Colors:
Antique rose, antique white, black, charcoal grey, honey brown, midnight blue, teal, terra cotta, and true ochre

Supplies:
Pine for rooster's body:
   12" wide x 10½" high x ¾" thick
Pine for rooster's wings:
   10" wide x 4" high x ³/₈" thick
Wooden dowel:
   (1) ½" diameter x 12" length
Stencil: ½" checks
Wood glue
Antique spray stain, golden oak
Matte spray varnish
Drill with ½" drill bit

1. Transfer patterns, cut out shapes, and sand and seal wood for painting. Refer to General Instructions on page 6 for a list of supplies needed and for detailed information on preparing wood for painting.

2. Refer to General Instructions on pages 6-8 for detailed information on painting techniques that are used for this project.

3. Paint both sides of rooster's body identically. Paint only one side of rooster's wings.

4. Antique rose: Paint rooster's wattle and comb.

5. Antique white: Paint rooster's body and wooden dowel.

6. Teal: Paint tail feathers.

7. Midnight blue: Paint rooster's wings.

8. True ochre: Paint rooster's beak.

9. Honey brown: Mix with a little antique white. Lightly stencil ½" checks on rooster's body.

10. Charcoal grey: Lightly stipple the upper front edges of rooster's wings. Spatter rooster.

11. Antique rose: Stipple rooster's cheeks.

12. Terra cotta: Lightly stipple eye area and outer edges of rooster's body.

13. Black: Apply dots for rooster's eyes. Spatter rooster's wings.

14. Sand edges of rooster's wings and lower part of body until unpainted wood is showing through.

15. Lightly spray outer edges with antique spray stain.

16. Using wood glue, glue rooster's wings to rooster as shown in photograph on page 17.

**Designed by
Debbie
Crabtree Lewis**

17. Finish with matte spray varnish.

18. Drill one ½" hole in bottom of rooster for placement of wooden dowel.

19. Using wood glue, glue wooden dowel inside hole in bottom of rooster. Allow glue to dry thoroughly. Photograph does not show wooden dowel.

Rooster's Body &
Rooster's Wings
- Enlarge 140%
- Cut 1 Rooster
- Cut 2 Wings
- Paint front & back of rooster's body
- Paint only one side of rooster's wings

Old Mac's Farm

Brushes:
Round fabric dye brush: #8
Flat brushes: #4, #8, #12
Liner brush: #2

Acrylic Paint Colors:
Beige, blue, Caucasian flesh, charcoal grey, dark green, gold, iron oxide, ivory, medium Caucasian flesh, and tan

Supplies:
Pine for base:
   $13^3/8$" wide x 10" high x $3/4$" thick
Pine for cut shapes:
   $13^3/8$" wide x 10" high x $3/8$" thick
Plywood for hay:
   2" x 2" x $1/8$" thick
Chicken wire: $11^1/4$" wide x 8" high
19-gauge wire:
   (4) 5" pieces
   (20) $3/4$" pieces
Wooden dowels:
   (2) $3/8$" diameter x $2^1/2$" length
Wooden beads:
   (2) 1" with $3/8$" openings
Stencil: $1/2$" checks
Linen jute: (1) 5" piece
4-ply jute: (1) 24" piece
Miniature cow bell
Industrial-strength glue
Wood glue
Antiquing medium
Clean cloth
Matte spray varnish
Hammer
Phillips screwdriver
Needlenose pliers
Drill with $1/16$" & $3/8$" drill bits

Designed by
Rebecca
Carter

1. Transfer patterns, cut out shapes, and sand and seal wood for painting. Refer to General Instructions on page 6 for a list of supplies needed and for detailed information on preparing wood for painting.

2. Refer to General Instructions on pages 6-8 for detailed information on painting techniques that are used for this project.

3. Ivory: Paint center area of base, rooster's body and head, cow's body and head, and top of silo. Paint back side of base.

4. Lay chicken wire across center area of base, making sure the heavier lines of the wire run against the wood grain. Hammer chicken wire against wood so chicken wire pattern is indented into wood. Remove chicken wire.

5. Tan: Paint border around base, cow's horns, silo, and wooden dowels.

6. Gold: Paint sun's rays and center, hay, and rooster's beak, legs, and feet.

7. Iron oxide: Stencil $1/2$" checks around border. Paint barn, barn door, and rooster's wattle and comb.

8. Medium Caucasian flesh: Paint pig's nose.

9. Caucasian flesh: Paint pig's body and head and cow's nose. Apply dots for pig's nostrils.

10. Beige: Paint patches in corners. Paint border around barn door.

11. Blue: Wash vertical and horizontal stripes on patches in corners and paint wooden beads.

12. Dark green: Paint barn roof and grass.

13. Charcoal grey: Wash vertical and horizontal stripes on patches in corners, making sure the checks are darker where the stripes intersect. Paint eyes, spots, and hooves on pig and cow and paint barn window. Paint eyes on rooster and apply dots for rooster's nostrils.

14. Iron oxide: Paint stripes on patches in corners.

15. Medium Caucasian flesh: Apply dots for cow's nostrils.

16. Sand edges of all wood pieces and randomly distress them using a hammer and a Phillips screwdriver.

17. Make 20 wire stitches from the $^3/_4$" pieces of 19-gauge wire. Bend both ends up like a "U" and hammer them into the wood as shown in photograph on page 20.

18. Finish with matte spray varnish.

19. Antique by applying antiquing medium to all wood pieces, making sure it gets deep into crevices made by the chicken wire and the Phillips screwdriver. Wipe off excess with a clean cloth.

20. Drill one $^3/_8$" hole in each side of base, measuring down 1" from top edge, for placement of wooden dowels. Drill one $^1/_{16}$" hole in top center of cow's head and pig's head for placement of wire bangs. Drill one $^1/_{16}$" hole in top center of cow's hips and pig's hips for placement of wire tails.

21. Using wood glue, glue animal body parts together: cow's head to cow's body, pig's head to pig's body, and rooster's head to rooster's body. Glue barn door and window to barn and glue hay to window. Glue sun's center to sun's rays. Insert wooden dowels inside wooden beads and glue in place. Glue wooden dowels inside drilled holes at top sides of base.

22. Take one 5" piece of 19-gauge wire. With needlenose pliers, grab one end of wire and twist it for bangs, leaving approximately 1" to glue into drilled hole in cow's head. Using industrial-strength glue, glue in place. Repeat for pig's bangs.

23. Take another 5" piece of 19-gauge wire. Curl it, leaving 3" straight to glue into drilled hole for cow's tail. Glue in place. Repeat for pig's tail, leaving only 1" straight to glue into drilled hole.

24. Thread linen jute through hole in cow bell and tie in a bow. Glue cow bell under cow's chin.

25. Using wood glue, glue cow, barn, pig, rooster, and sun to top of base as shown in photograph.

26. Spray with matte spray varnish again.

27. Tie 4-ply jute around wooden dowels for hanging.

Old Mac's Farm
- Enlarge 150%
- Cut 1 Base
- Cut 1 Cow's Head
- Cut 1 Cow's Body
- Cut 1 Pig's Head
- Cut 1 Pig's Body
- Cut 1 Rooster's Head
- Cut 1 Rooster's Body
- Cut 1 Barn with Silo
- Cut 1 Barn Door
- Cut 1 Window
- Cut 1 Hay Shape
- Cut 1 Sun
- Cut 1 Sun's Center
- Paint front & back of base — back side is not detail painted
- Paint only one side of all shapes

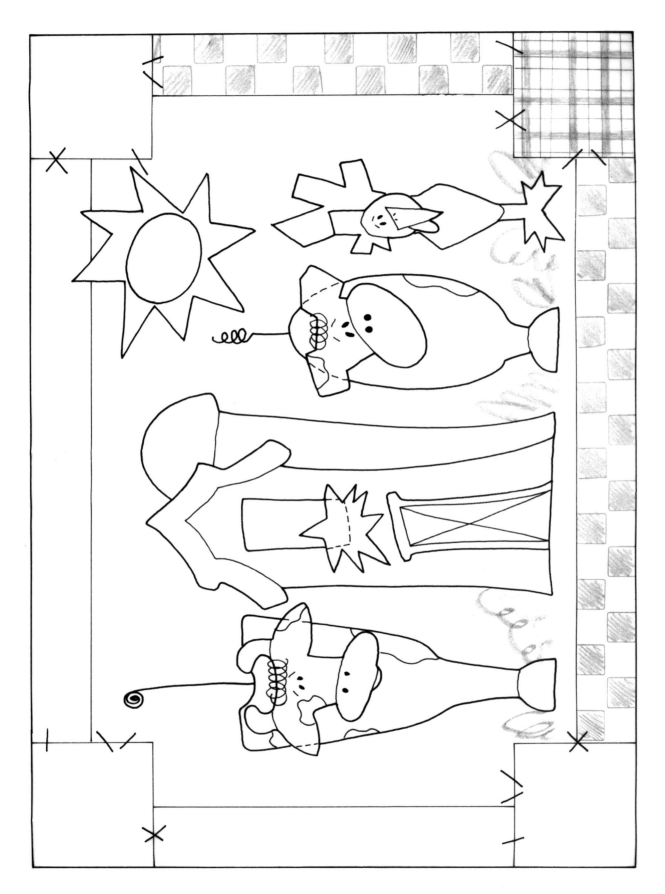

Guardian Bunny

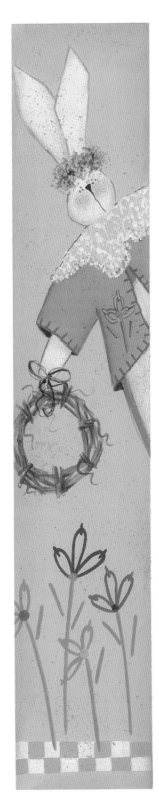

Designed by
Rebecca
Carter

Brushes:
Round fabric dye brush: #2
Flat brushes: #2, #4, #8
Liner brush: #2

Acrylic Paint Colors:
Antique white, blue-grey, blush, burnt orange, charcoal grey, colonial blue, dark purple, honey brown, light avocado, light green, sand, and true ochre

Supplies:
Pine for bunny:
   $5^1/2$" wide x 14" high x $^3/4$" thick
Pine for bunny's arms & legs:
   7" wide x 5" high x $^1/2$" thick
Pine for bunny's top ear & apron:
   5" wide x 8" high x $^1/4$" thick
19-gauge wire: (4) 4" pieces
Plush felt fabric:
   Light brown: (1) 10" x 12"
Embroidery floss:
   blue, gold, light green, orange
Round doily: (1) 4" diameter
Plastic button: (1) 1"
Linen jute: $3^1/2$ yards
Wreath: (1) $3^1/2$" diameter
Papier-mâché birdhouse:
   (1) 3" wide x 3" high
Spanish moss
Twigs: Approximately 15" in length
Craft glue
Industrial-strength glue
Wood glue
Antiquing medium
Clean cloth
Antique spray stain, golden oak
Matte spray varnish

Needlenose pliers
Drill with $^1/16$" drill bit
Needle
Scissors
Matching thread
Sewing machine

1. Transfer patterns, cut out shapes, and sand and seal wood for painting. Refer to General Instructions on page 6 for a list of supplies needed and for detailed information on preparing wood for painting.

2. Refer to General Instructions on pages 6-8 for detailed information on painting techniques that are used for this project.

3. Antique white: Paint bunny's face, ears, arms, and legs. Paint bunny's apron and birdhouse. Paint back sides of all wood pieces, except bunny's apron.

4. Honey brown: Paint bunny's dress.

5. Light avocado: Wash wide plaid stripes on bunny's dress.

6. Sand: Paint border on bunny's apron.

7. Blue-grey: Paint birdhouse's roof.

8. Colonial blue: Paint checks on border of bunny's apron.

9. Blush: Paint narrow stripes on each side of wide plaid stripes on bunny's dress. Dry-brush bunny's cheeks and paint flowers on bunny's apron and on birdhouse as shown in pattern on page 27.

10. Charcoal grey: Wash border around birdhouse. Wash checks on border darker. Paint bunny's face.

11. Light green: Paint flower stems and leaves using a #2 liner brush on bunny's apron and on birdhouse.

12. Dark purple: Paint purple-colored flowers as shown in photograph on page 24.

13. True ochre: Paint yellow-colored flowers as shown in photograph.

14. Burnt orange: Paint orange-colored flowers as shown in photograph.

15. Apply dots for flower centers in a variety of colors as shown in photograph.

16. Sand edges of all wood pieces.

17. Finish with matte spray varnish.

18. Antique by applying antiquing medium to all wood pieces. Wipe off excess with a clean cloth.

19. Using wood glue, glue apron on bunny.

20. Drill 1/16" holes in tops of bunny's arms and legs, in bunny's hands, and at top and bottom of bunny's dress. Assemble bunny with 4" pieces of 19-gauge wire.

21. Lightly spray birdhouse with antique spray stain.

22. Cut two fronts and one back piece (on the fold) for jacket from plush felt fabric. Sew, right sides together, at shoulder and side seams. Turn right side out.

23. Blanket-stitch around edges and sleeves with orange embroidery floss as shown on page 27.

24. Stitch stems and leaves with light green embroidery floss.

25. Use the lazy-daisy stitch to make flowers with blue embroidery floss as shown on page 27.

26. Stitch French knots for flower centers with gold embroidery floss.

27. Slip jacket on bunny. Cut doily up the back and wrap it around bunny's neck. Using industrial-strength glue, glue it in the back.

28. Thread linen jute through holes in 1" plastic button and tie in a bow. Using craft glue, glue it on top of doily collar.

29. Thread linen jute through birdhouse roof and through hole in bunny's hand and tie a knot. Wrap linen jute around wreath two or three times, thread through hole in other bunny's hand, and tie a knot.

30. Using craft glue, glue Spanish moss around bottom of bunny's ears. Tie a loopy linen jute bow and glue it to side of bunny's head.

31. Make two bundles of twigs for wings that measure approximately 15" in length. Secure by wrapping them in the center with linen jute. Using industrial-strength glue, glue wings to back of bunny's jacket.

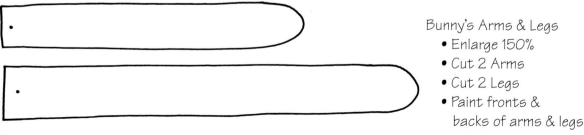

Bunny's Arms & Legs
- Enlarge 150%
- Cut 2 Arms
- Cut 2 Legs
- Paint fronts & backs of arms & legs

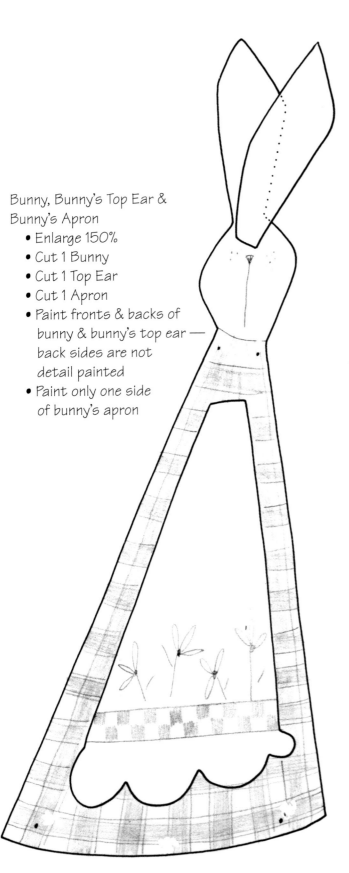

Bunny, Bunny's Top Ear &
Bunny's Apron
- Enlarge 150%
- Cut 1 Bunny
- Cut 1 Top Ear
- Cut 1 Apron
- Paint fronts & backs of
  bunny & bunny's top ear —
  back sides are not
  detail painted
- Paint only one side
  of bunny's apron

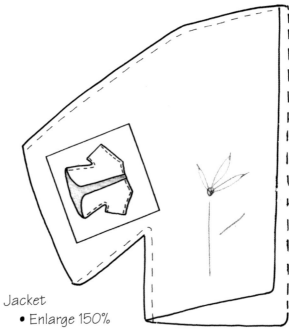

Jacket
- Enlarge 150%
- Cut 2 Fronts
- Cut 1 Back
- Sew seams
  right sides together
- Use $1/4"$ seam allowance
- Embellish with
  embroidery floss

Blanket Stitch

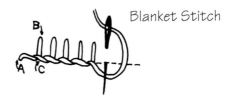

Lazy Daisy Stitch

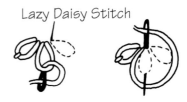

27

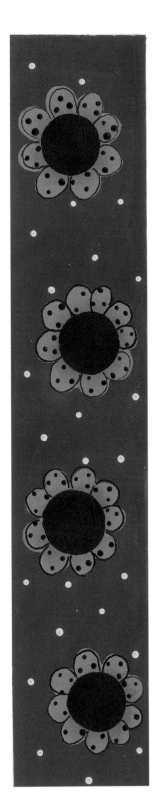

Country Girl

Brushes:
Round fabric dye brush: #6
Flat brushes:
    #1, #2, #4, #6, #8, #10
Liner brush: #00

Acrylic Paint Colors:
Beige, black, brick red, burnt sienna, coral, country blue, forest green, gold, ivory, light blue, light coral, light green, midnight blue, and white

Supplies:
Pine for girl:
    10" wide x 15" high x $^3/_4$" thick
Pine for flower garland:
    $9^1/_2$" wide x $3^1/_2$" high x $^1/_2$" thick
Pine for collar:
    6" wide x $2^1/_2$" high x $^1/_4$" thick
Wooden buttons: (1) $^3/_4$", (3) 1"
19-gauge wire: (1) 9" piece
Curly crepe wool doll hair, red
Straw hat: (1) 6" diameter
Linen jute: (3) 9" pieces
Scraps of fabric
Eye hooks: (2) $^1/_4$"
Raffia
Permanent black marker,
    fine-point
Glue gun & glue sticks,
    low temperature
Industrial-strength glue
Wood glue
Antique spray stain, golden oak
Matte spray varnish
Needlenose pliers
Drill with $^1/_{16}$" drill bit

1. Transfer patterns, cut out shapes, and sand and seal wood for painting. Refer to General Instructions on page 6 for a list of supplies needed and for detailed information on preparing wood for painting.

2. Refer to General Instructions on pages 6-8 for detailed information on painting techniques that are used for this project.

3. Light coral: Paint girl's face and hands.

4. Beige: Paint sleeves on dress.

5. Ivory: Paint girl's legs and collar. Paint back side of girl.

6. Brick red: Paint apron on dress. Paint plaid pattern on sleeves using a #4 flat brush and thinned paint. Paint vertical stripes first and then paint horizontal stripes.

7. Midnight blue: Paint dress.

8. Coral: Stipple girl's cheeks.

9. Forest green: Paint leaves on flower garland and grassy area around girl's feet.

10. Country blue: Paint morning-glories on flower garland.

11. Gold: Paint sunflowers on flower garland.

**Designed by
Debbie
Crabtree Lewis**

12. Light blue: Stipple morning-glory centers.

13. Burnt sienna: Stipple sunflower centers, larger than a one inch area.

14. Light green: Paint plaid pattern on leaves using a #1 flat brush and thinned paint.

15. Black: Apply dots on sunflowers and apply dots for girl's eyes. Paint shoes and all four wooden buttons.

16. White: Apply dots on morning-glory centers.

17. Ivory: Apply dots on dress and paint stitches on apron. Paint back sides of collar and flower garland.

18. Line around dress, sleeves, collar, sunflowers, morning-glories, leaves, girl's hands, and legs with fine-point permanent black marker. Apply dots for freckles.

19. Finish with matte spray varnish because of linework.

20. Lightly spray outer edges of girl, collar, and flower garland with antique spray stain, avoiding girl's face.

21. Sand edges of dress, 3/4" wooden button, and grassy area around girl's feet until unpainted wood is showing through.

22. Using wood glue, glue collar to girl's neck and glue 3/4" wooden button to center of collar.

23. Drill one 1/16" hole in each side of flower garland.

24. Screw eye hooks into drilled holes on flower garland.

25. Thread raffia through eye hooks on each side of flower garland and tie into bows.

26. Thread linen jute through holes in 1" wooden buttons and tie into bows. Using wood glue, glue wooden buttons to sunflower centers.

27. Bend the 19-gauge wire into eye glasses with needlenose pliers, leaving 1"-long tails on each side. Bend the wire tails facing backward and, using industrial-strength glue, glue eye glasses to girl's face.

28. Using a low temperature glue gun and glue sticks, glue doll hair around top of girl's head. No hair needs to be glued to back of head.

29. Glue straw hat to girl's head.

30. Tie scraps of fabric into a bow and glue into hair at side of girl's head.

31. Using wood glue, glue flower garland across front of girl from hand to hand.

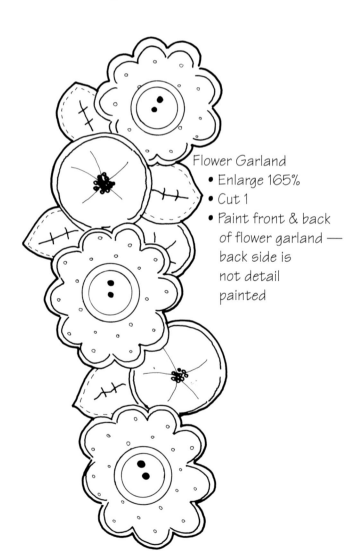

Flower Garland
• Enlarge 165%
• Cut 1
• Paint front & back of flower garland — back side is not detail painted

Collar
- Enlarge 165%
- Cut 1
- Paint front & back of collar — back side is not detail painted

Country Girl
- Enlarge 165%
- Cut 1
- Paint front & back of country girl — back side is not detail painted

31

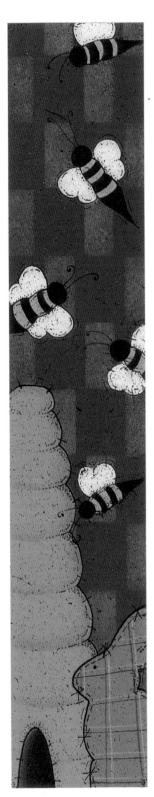

**Designed by
Jill
Webster**

Welcome Bee Keeper

Brushes:
Round fabric dye brush: #14
Flat brushes: #8, #12, #16
Liner brush: #6/0

Acrylic Paint Colors:
Antique gold, antique white, avocado, black, Caucasian flesh, country blue, cranberry, dark forest green, dark green, dark plum, honey brown, khaki tan, medium green, midnight blue, raspberry, and raw sienna

Stencil Cream Colors:
Burgundy and red iron oxide

Supplies:
Pine for base:
    11" wide x $7^1/4$" high x $3/4$" thick
Pine for bee keeper &
bee keeper's arms:
    11" wide x 36" high x $3/4$" thick
Pine for beehives:
    $9^1/2$ wide" x 10" high x $3/4$" thick
Pine for bunny:
    6" wide x 9" high x $3/4$" thick
Pine for four bees:
    $1^1/2$" wide x 6" high x $1/8$" thick
Pine for three bees:
    $1^1/2$" wide x 6" high x $1/4$" thick
Chalkboard: (1) $7^1/2$" wide x $5^1/2$" high
Stencils: $1/4$" checks, $1/2$" checks &
    $1/4$" wide x $5/8$" high rectangles
19-gauge wire, black: 3 yards &
    (6) 31" pieces
27-gauge wire: $1^1/2$ yards
Tube: (1) 2" diameter
Plush felt fabric:
    Dark blue:
        (1) 10" x 20"
        (1) $2^1/4$" x 3"

Felt fabric:
    Mustard: 3" x $4^1/2$"
    Dark green: $5^1/2$" x $2^1/2$"
Plastic buttons: (2) Large, (1) Small
Doll hair, curly red
Straw hat: (1) 7" diameter
Silk or dried flowers, greenery,
    and berries
Linen jute: 3 yards
Clean cloth
Permanent black marker,
    fine-point
Glue gun & glue sticks,
    low temperature
Industrial-strength glue
Wood glue
Antique spray stain, golden oak
Matte spray varnish
Needlenose pliers
Drill with $1/16$" drill bit
Needle
Scissors
Matching thread
Sewing machine
Router

1.   Transfer patterns, cut out shapes, and sand and seal wood for painting. Refer to General Instructions on page 6 for a list of supplies needed and for detailed information on preparing wood for painting. Rout top edge of base to round.

2.   Refer to General Instructions on pages 6-8 for detailed information on painting techniques that are used for this project.

3. Dark green: Paint base.

4. Medium green: Stipple base.

5. Spray outer edges with antique spray stain.

6. Antique white: Paint bees' wings.

7. Antique gold: Paint center of bees.

8. Black: Paint bees' heads and stripes.

9. Line bees with fine-point permanent black marker.

10. Spray bees with antique spray stain.

11. Honey brown: Paint beehives.

12. Honey brown: Mix with a little antique white. Dry-brush down centers of beehives.

13. Raw sienna: Float-shade beehives.

14. Black: Paint doors on beehives.

15. Line beehives with fine-point permanent black marker.

16. Spray beehives with antique spray stain, spraying the edges a little heavier.

17. Dark forest green: Paint bunny.

18. Khaki tan: Apply dots on bunny.

19. Finish bunny with matte spray varnish.

20. Tie a linen jute bow around bunny's neck.

21. Cranberry: Paint chalkboard center.

22. Antique white: Paint chalkboard frame.

23. Raspberry: Stencil 1/2" checks on chalkboard center.

24. Khaki tan: Paint lettering on chalkboard center.

25. Raw sienna: Float-shade around outside edges of chalkboard.

26. Line chalkboard and lettering with fine-point permanent black marker.

27. Spray chalkboard with antique spray stain, spraying the edges a little heavier.

28. Caucasian flesh: Paint bee keeper's face, hands, and legs.

29. Dark forest green: Paint top section of bee keeper's dress and sleeves.

30. Medium green: Stipple top section of dress and sleeves.

31. Dark green: Float-shade around neckline and down center front of dress.

32. Avocado: Stencil rectangles on dress and sleeves.

33. Antique white: Paint a thin line around neckline and down center front of dress to the left of where buttons will be painted. Paint stripes between the bands on dress and sleeves.

34. Midnight blue: Paint the top bands on bottom section of dress and sleeves.

35. Dark plum: Paint the bottom bands on bottom section of dress and sleeves.

36. Country blue: Paint stripes on midnight blue bands on dress and sleeves.

37. Raspberry: Stipple 1/4" checks on dark plum bands on dress and sleeves.

38. Antique gold: Paint beehives on midnight blue band on dress and paint buttons down center front of dress.

39. Honey brown: Paint lines down and across the beehives on midnight blue band on dress.

40. Line these beehives with fine-point permanent black marker.

41. Khaki tan: Paint criss-cross stitches on beehives.

42. Antique white: Paint running stitches on the tops and the bottoms of midnight blue and dark plum bands on dress and sleeves.

43. Khaki tan: Paint bunnies on dark plum band on dress and paint bee keeper's socks.

44. Black: Paint doors on beehives and paint bee keeper's shoes.

45. Avocado: Paint bunny at left on dark plum band, leaving a khaki tan border.

46. Antique gold: Paint thin lines down bunny.

47. Dark plum: Paint thin lines across bunny.

48. Midnight blue: Paint thin lines under the dark plum lines across bunny.

49. Line stitches around outside edge of avocado-colored bunny with fine-point permanent black marker.

50. Midnight blue: Paint bunny second from left, leaving a khaki tan border.

51. Khaki tan: Apply dots on bunny.

52. Line stitches around outside edge of midnight blue-colored bunny with fine-point permanent black marker.

53. Dark green: Paint bunny second from right, leaving a khaki tan border.

54. Medium green: Paint thin, single lines down and across bunny.

55. Antique gold: Paint thin, triple lines down bunny.

56. Midnight blue: Paint thin lines between every other single medium green line across bunny.

57. Dark plum: Paint thin lines between every other single medium green line across bunny.

58. Line stitches around outside edge of dark green-colored bunny with fine-point permanent black marker.

59. Medium green: Paint bunny at right, leaving a khaki tan border.

60. Avocado: Paint thin, double lines across bunny.

61. Dark green: Paint thin, single lines down and across bunny.

62. Dark plum: Paint thin lines down left side of dark green lines.

63. Line stitches around outside edge of medium green-colored bunny with fine-point permanent black marker.

64. Khaki tan: Paint criss-cross stitches on bunnies across dark plum band on dress.

65. Black: Apply dots on buttons.

66. Line stitches to bee keeper's dress, sleeves, and socks with fine-point permanent black marker.

67. Khaki tan: Paint a thin line down center of bee keeper's shoes to divide them.

68. Lightly sand top edges of bee keeper's shoes.

69. Stipple over bee keeper's face, hands, and legs with red iron oxide stencil cream. Wipe off as much as possible with a clean cloth, leaving a little excess under bee keeper's chin.

70. Stipple bee keeper's cheeks with burgundy stencil cream.

71. Black: Apply dots for bee keeper's eyes.

72. Line bee keeper's face, hands, and legs with fine-point permanent black marker. Line stitches and details on bee keeper's dress.

73. Spray bee keeper with antique spray stain, spraying the edges a little heavier.

74. Drill $1/16$" holes in tops of bee keeper's arms and at top of bee keeper's dress. Assemble bee keeper with 19-gauge wire.

75. Drill $1/16$" hole through (from side to side) top of tall beehive and through bee keeper's hands. Drill $1/16$" holes in top corners of chalkboard.

76. Using wood glue, glue bee keeper to base.

77. Cut two fronts and one back piece (on the fold) for vest from dark blue plush felt fabric. Sew, right sides together, at shoulder and side seams. Turn right side out.

78. Blanket-stitch around edges of vest with linen jute as shown on page 27. Blanket-stitch heart, star, and pocket into place on front of vest.

79. Sew buttons on vest as shown in photograph on page 32.

80. Using industrial-strength glue, glue one $\frac{1}{8}$"-thick bee to front of vest pocket.

81. Slip vest on bee keeper.

82. Using 19-gauge wire, wire tall beehive to bee keeper's right hand and wire chalkboard to bee keeper's left hand.

83. Using wood glue, glue remaining beehive to base in front of bee keeper as shown in photograph. Glue bunny to base in front of bee keeper across from beehive.

84. Glue one $\frac{1}{4}$"-thick bee to tall beehive hanging from bee keeper's right hand. Glue one $\frac{1}{8}$"-thick bee to side of beehive glued to base. Glue remaining $\frac{1}{8}$"-thick bees to chalkboard frame.

85. Drill a $\frac{1}{16}$" hole on top front edge of base near beehive and a $\frac{1}{16}$" hole on the underside of one $\frac{1}{4}$"-thick bee.

86. Curl a piece of 19-gauge wire and, using industrial-strength glue, glue one end into drilled hole in base and the other end into drilled hole on underside of bee.

87. Tie doll hair into bunches 2" long for bangs. Using a low temperature glue gun and glue sticks, glue bangs into place. Tie doll hair into bunches 5" long. Glue hair into place around bee keeper's head.

88. Glue straw hat to top back of bee keeper's head and trim doll hair to shoulder length.

89. Glue an arrangement of silk or dried flowers, greenery, and berries to the brim of bee keeper's hat.

90. Glue the remaining $\frac{1}{4}$"-thick bee to the front of bee keeper's hat.

91. Finish all wood pieces with matte spray varnish.

92. Each wing is made from the six 31" pieces of 19-gauge wire. Wrap the middle of the wire around a 2" tube and fold the wire in half. Make three wings for each side and wire the sets of three together, overlapping in the center by at least one inch. Wrap the 27-gauge wire around all six wings to secure.

93. Wrap the $2\frac{1}{4}$" x 3" piece of dark blue plush felt over the center of the wings and glue tightly in place.

94. Hand-stitch felt onto center back of vest.

95. To secure wings, glue back of vest to back of bee keeper.

Bunny
• Enlarge 230%
• Cut 1
• Paint front & back of bunny

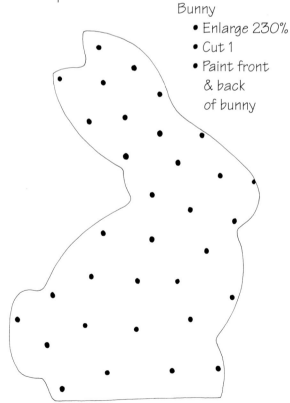

Beehive
- Enlarge 130%
- Cut 1
- Paint front
  & back
  of beehive

Tall Beehive
- Enlarge 130%
- Cut 1
- Paint front
  & back
  of tall beehive

Bees
- Reproduce
  at 100%
- Cut 4 from
  1/8"-thick pine
- Cut 3 from
  1/4"-thick pine
- Paint fronts
  & backs
  of bees

37

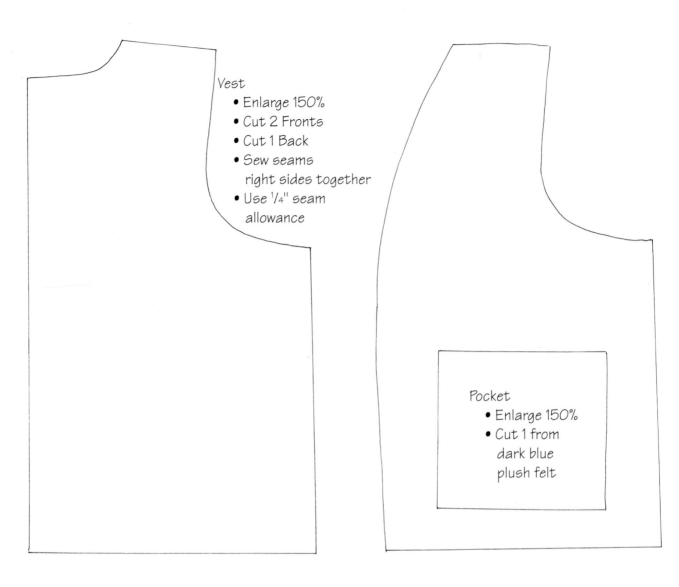

Vest
- Enlarge 150%
- Cut 2 Fronts
- Cut 1 Back
- Sew seams right sides together
- Use 1/4" seam allowance

Pocket
- Enlarge 150%
- Cut 1 from dark blue plush felt

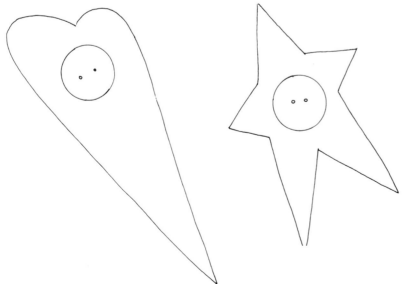

Heart & Star
- Enlarge 150%
- Cut 1 Heart from dark green felt
- Cut 1 Star from mustard felt
- Patterns show button placement

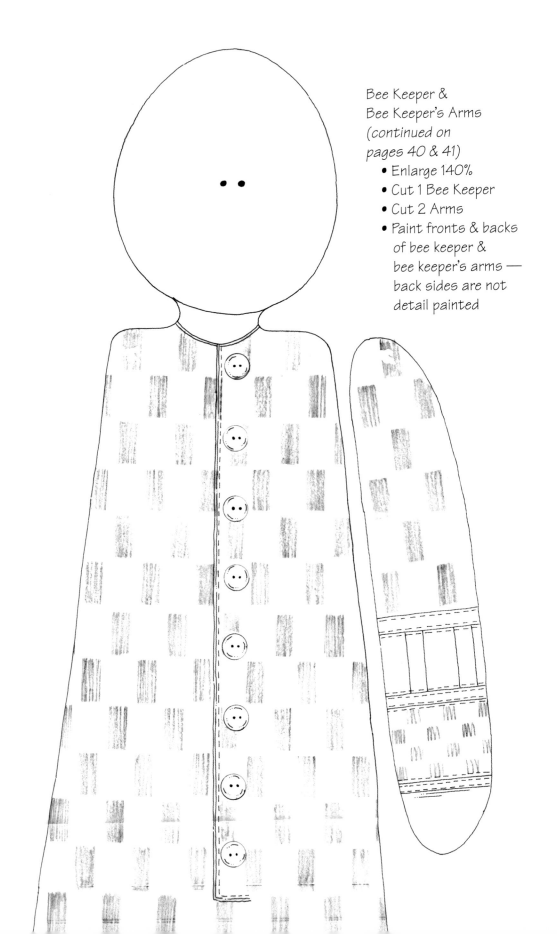

Bee Keeper &
Bee Keeper's Arms
(continued on
pages 40 & 41)
- Enlarge 140%
- Cut 1 Bee Keeper
- Cut 2 Arms
- Paint fronts & backs
  of bee keeper &
  bee keeper's arms —
  back sides are not
  detail painted

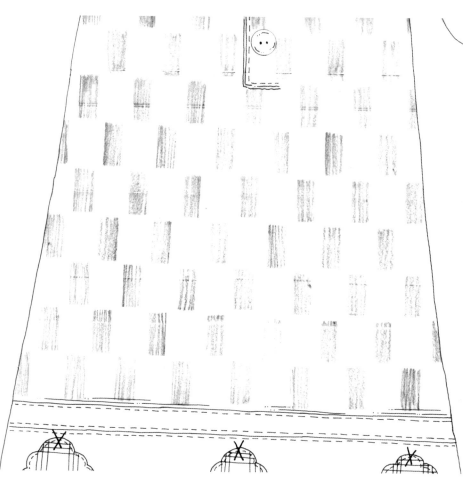

Bee Keeper
(*continued from
page 39 and on page 41*)
- Enlarge 140%
- Cut 1
- Paint front
  & back
  of bee keeper —
  back side is
  not detail
  painted

Chalkboard
- Enlarge 180%
- Paint only one
  side of chalkboard
- Paint front &
  back of
  chalkboard frame

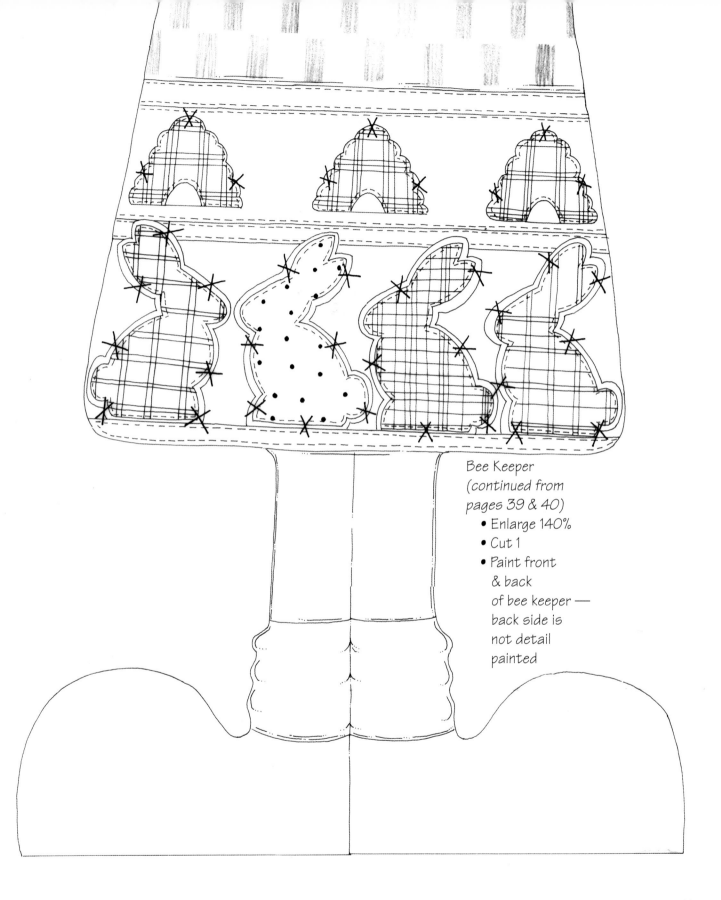

Bee Keeper
(continued from
pages 39 & 40)
• Enlarge 140%
• Cut 1
• Paint front
  & back
  of bee keeper —
  back side is
  not detail
  painted

Cock-A-Doodle-Doo Chalkboard

Brushes:
Flat brushes: #2, #4, #8
Liner brush: #2

Acrylic Paint Colors:
Antique white, burnt orange, charcoal grey, country blue, cream, honey brown, khaki tan, light avocado, midnight blue, and wine

Supplies:
Chalkboard: (1) 6" wide x 8" high
Antique spray stain, golden oak
Matte spray varnish

1. Refer to General Instructions on pages 6-8 for detailed information on painting techniques that are used for this project.

Top Left Square:

2. Wine: Paint square.

3. Country blue: Wash vertical and horizontal stripes. Paint chalkboard frame.

4. Charcoal grey: Wash the narrow vertical and horizontal stripes.

5. Cream: Paint chicken.

6. Burnt orange: Paint chicken's wattle and comb.

7. Honey brown: Paint chicken's beak and feet.

8. Light avocado: Apply dots on chicken.

Top Right Square:

9. Antique white: Paint square.

10. Khaki tan: Paint stars.

11. Light avocado: Paint chicken.

12. Midnight blue: Wash vertical and horizontal stripes. Darken squares where stripes intersect.

13. Wine: Wash the vertical and horizontal stripes.

14. Burnt orange: Paint chicken's wattle and comb.

15. Charcoal grey: Paint chicken's beak and feet.

Bottom Left Square:

16. Khaki tan: Paint square.

17. Midnight blue: Paint stars.

18. Burnt orange: Paint chicken.

19. Honey brown: Wash vertical and horizontal stripes. Paint checks where stripes intersect.

20. Charcoal grey: Wash the vertical and horizontal stripes.

21. Wine: Paint chicken's wattle and comb.

22. Light avocado: Paint chicken's beak and feet.

Bottom Right Square:

23. Honey brown: Paint square.

24. Light avocado: Wash vertical and horizontal stripes.

Designed by Rebecca Carter

43

25. Midnight blue: Wash the vertical and horizontal stripes.

26. Charcoal grey: Paint chicken.

27. Wine: Paint chicken's wattle and comb.

28. Burnt orange: Paint chicken's beak and feet.

29. Cream: Apply dots on chicken.

Top Stripe:

30. Wine: Paint stripe.

31. Burnt orange: Wash vertical and horizontal stripes. Darken squares.

32. Midnight blue: Wash vertical and horizontal stripes.

33. Cream: Paint lettering using a #2 liner brush.

Bottom Stripe:

34. Light avocado: Paint stripe.

35. Midnight blue: Paint triangles.

36. Honey brown: Paint chicken feet.

37. Charcoal grey: Paint stitches around each square and around top and bottom stripes.

38. Finish with matte spray varnish.

39. Spray outer edges with antique spray stain.

40. Spray with matte spray varnish again.

41. To display, set on a shelf or on an easel.

Chalkboard
- Enlarge 115%
- Paint only one side of chalkboard
- Paint front & back of chalkboard frame

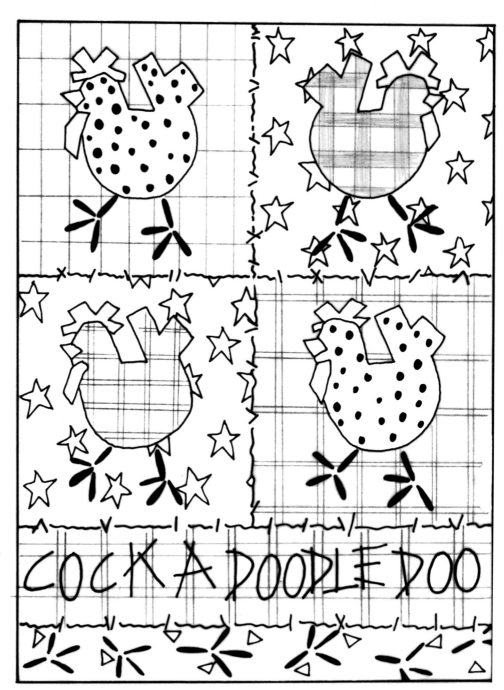

Barnyard Friends
Chalkboard

Barnyard Friends Chalkboard

Brushes:
Flat brushes: #2, #4, #8, #12
Liner brush: #2

Acrylic Paint Colors:
Antique gold, antique white, brick red, burnt orange, Caucasian flesh, charcoal grey, colonial blue, cream, honey brown, khaki tan, and light avocado

Supplies:
Chalkboard: (1) 6" wide x 8" high
14-gauge wire: (1) 22" piece
Plastic buttons: (3) 1/2"
Linen jute: (3) 4" pieces
Permanent black marker,
    fine-point
Permanent brown marker,
    fine-point
Industrial-strength glue
Sandpaper, fine-grit
Antiquing medium
Clean cloth
Antique spray stain, golden oak
Matte spray varnish
Needlenose pliers
Drill with 1/8" drill bit

1. Refer to General Instructions on pages 6-8 for detailed information on painting techniques that are used for this project.

2. Antique white: Paint chalkboard.

3. Khaki tan: Paint stars.

4. Honey brown: Paint top patch and birdhouse's pole.

5. Burnt orange: Paint bottom patch and birdhouse.

6. Brick red: Paint second patch, flag at top of birdhouse, heart at bottom of birdhouse's pole, and checks on birdhouse.

7. Light avocado: Paint third patch and birdhouse's roof.

8. Colonial blue: Paint chalkboard frame.

9. Cream: Paint checks around chalkboard frame. Paint rooster.

10. Antique white: Paint sheep and cow.

11. Antique gold: Paint sunflowers. Paint rooster's beak and feet.

12. Burnt orange: Paint rooster's wattle and comb.

13. Burnt orange: Mix with a little Caucasian flesh. Paint pig and cow's udder. Add a little more burnt orange and paint pig's back legs.

14. Charcoal grey: Paint the sheep's face, ear, and legs. Paint cow's spots. Paint arrow across birdhouse's pole and hole on birdhouse. Apply dot at top of birdhouse flag pole. Paint stitches around patches.

**Designed by
Rebecca
Carter**

15. Sand edges of chalkboard frame.

16. Line stitches around sunflowers with fine-point permanent black marker.

17. Line lettering with fine-point permanent brown marker.

18. Finish with matte spray varnish because of linework.

19. Antique by applying antiquing medium. Wipe off excess with a clean cloth.

20. Thread linen jute through holes in buttons and tie into bows.

21. Using industrial-strength glue, glue buttons to sunflower centers.

22. Spray outer edges of chalkboard frame with antique spray stain.

23. Spray with matte spray varnish again.

24. Drill one $1/8$" hole in each corner at top of chalkboard frame.

25. Curl 14-gauge wire, leaving $1 1/2$" ends straight. Thread straight ends through drilled holes in chalkboard frame and bend upward to secure for hanging.

Chalkboard
- Enlarge 115%
- Paint only one side of chalkboard
- Paint front & back of chalkboard frame

Ladybug Windmill

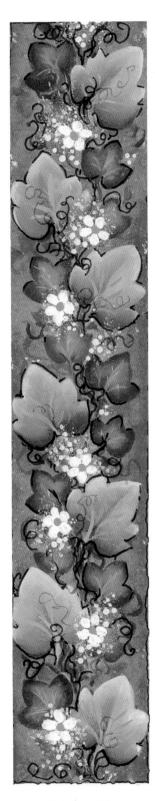

Designed by Emily Dinsdale

Brushes:
Flat brushes: #6, #10
Liner brush: #1

Acrylic Paint Colors:
Black, blush, bright orange, Caucasian flesh, dark red, evergreen, jade green, light cinnamon, medium green, snow white, straw, terra cotta, true ochre, and yellow

Supplies:
Pine for ladybug's body:
    4" wide x 5" high x ¼" thick
Plywood for sleeves & windmill leaves:
    5" wide x 6" high x ⅛" thick
19-gauge wire, black:
    (2) 3" pieces
Wooden dowel:
    (1) ⅛" diameter x 12" length
Windmill assembly:
    Wooden dowel:
        (1) ⅜" diameter x 1" length
    Wooden hub:
        (1) 1" diameter x ⅜" thick
    Round-head wood screw:
        (1) #4 x 1"
Permanent black marker,
    fine-point
Permanent brown marker,
    fine-point
Industrial-strength glue
Wood glue
Matte spray varnish
Needlenose pliers
Drill with ³/₃₂", ¹/₁₆",
    ⅛" & ⅜" drill bits

1. Transfer patterns, cut out shapes, and sand and seal wood for painting. Refer to General Instructions on page 6 for a list of supplies needed and for detailed information on preparing wood for painting.

2. Refer to General Instructions on pages 6-8 for detailed information on painting techniques that are used for this project.

3. Caucasian flesh: Paint ladybug's face, feet, and tiny parts of hands.

4. Bright orange: Paint ladybug's dress on both sides.

5. Jade green: Paint ladybug's underskirt on front and sleeves on both sides of both wood pieces.

6. Black: Paint spots on ladybug's dress on both sides. Paint bodice of dress and shoes on both sides. Apply dots for eyes.

7. Straw: Paint flower's center.

8. Medium green: Paint leaves and stem on flower and paint all four windmill leaves on both sides. Float-shade across bottom of underskirt and on ladybug's elbows.

9. Snow white: Paint flower.

10. True ochre: Paint ladybug's hair on both sides and float-shade lower edge of flower's center.

11. Blush: Float-shade ladybug's cheeks and across bottom of face and chin. Paint ladybug's lips.

12. Bright orange: Paint ladybugs' wings on two windmill leaves.

13. Dark red: Float-shade around inside edges of ladybug's dress on both sides and around edges of ladybugs' wings on windmill leaves.

14. Terra cotta: Float-shade ladybug's hair on both sides and apply dot "freckles" to ladybug's cheeks.

15. Light cinnamon: Float-shade across ladybug's bun and around the curls outlining ladybug's face. Wash 12" length of wooden dowel.

16. Yellow: Apply dots on flower's center.

17. Evergreen: Float-shade leaves and stem on flower and all four windmill leaves.

18. Jade green: Line leaves and stem on flower.

19. Black: Paint heads, bodies, spots, and antennae on the ladybugs on windmill leaves. Paint wooden dowel and hub for windmill assembly.

20. Snow white: Apply dots in ladybug's eyes. Lightly float-shade over nose, under mouth, and across forehead.

21. Line curls in ladybug's hair on both sides, stripes on underskirt, flower petals and stem, and ladybug's eyelashes with fine-point permanent black marker.

22. Line ladybug's nose, mouth, and eyebrows with fine-point permanent brown marker.

23. Finish with matte spray varnish because of linework.

24. Drill one 1/16" hole in bottom center of ladybug's bun for placement of antennae. Drill one

1/8" hole in bottom of ladybug's feet for placement of wooden dowel. Drill one 3/8" hole through center back of ladybug's bodice for placement of wooden dowel for windmill assembly.

25. Using wood glue, glue sleeves to ladybug to cover drilled hole as shown in photograph on page 48. Glue wooden dowel inside hole in bottom of ladybug's feet.

26. Take both pieces of 19-gauge wire and curl for antennae. Using industrial-strength glue, glue one end of each antennae into drilled hole in ladybug's bun. Position antennae as desired.

27. Assemble windmill. Refer to General Instructions on page 9 for detailed information and diagrams on assembling small windmills.

28. Using wood glue, glue windmill assembly into back of ladybug. Allow glue to dry thoroughly.

Ladybug's Sleeves
• Reproduce at 100%
• Cut 1
• Paint front & back of ladybug's sleeves — back side is not detail painted

Windmill Leaves
• Reproduce at 100%
• Cut 4
• Paint fronts & backs of windmill leaves
• Paint ladybugs on 2 windmill leaves

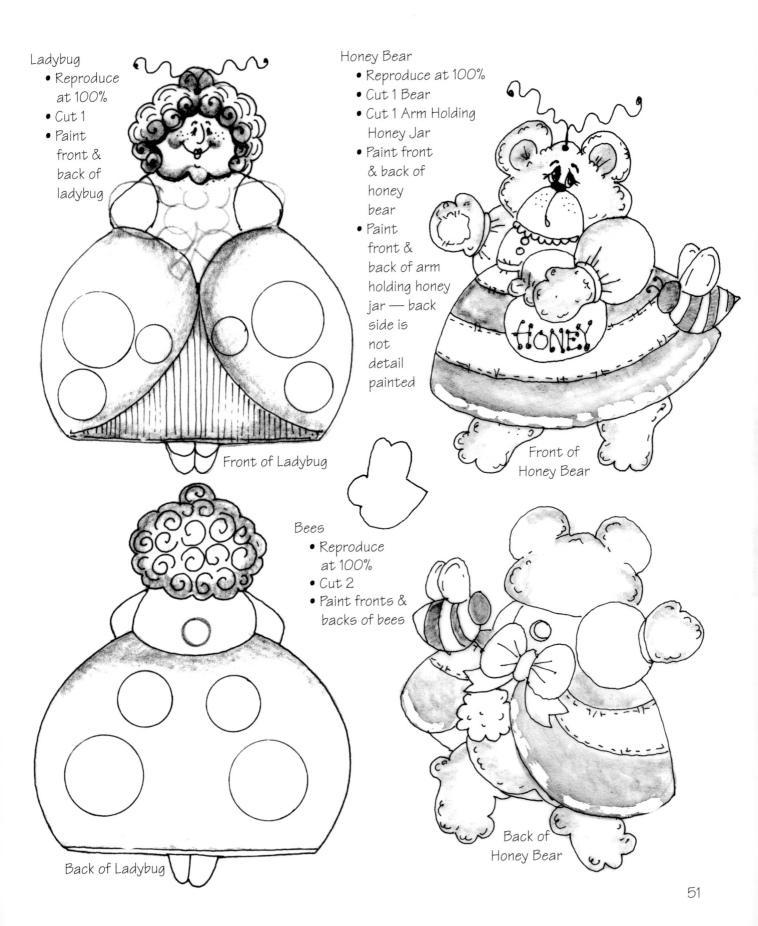

Ladybug
- Reproduce at 100%
- Cut 1
- Paint front & back of ladybug

Front of Ladybug

Honey Bear
- Reproduce at 100%
- Cut 1 Bear
- Cut 1 Arm Holding Honey Jar
- Paint front & back of honey bear
- Paint front & back of arm holding honey jar — back side is not detail painted

HONEY

Front of Honey Bear

Bees
- Reproduce at 100%
- Cut 2
- Paint fronts & backs of bees

Back of Ladybug

Back of Honey Bear

51

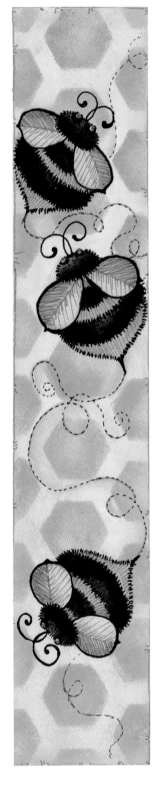

Honey Bear Windmill

Patterns on pages 51 & 54.

Brushes:
Flat brush: #6
Liner brush: #1

Acrylic Paint Colors:
Black, chocolate, clay, country blue, light buttermilk, light cinnamon, mink, sable, snow white, straw, taffy, toffee, and true ochre

Supplies:
Pine for honey bear's body:
   4" wide x 5" high x ¼" thick
Plywood for arm holding honey jar,
   bees & windmill wings:
   7" wide x 4" high x ⅛" thick
19-gauge wire, black:
   (2) 3" pieces
Wooden dowel:
   (1) ⅛" diameter x 12" length
Windmill assembly:
   Wooden dowel:
      (1) ⅜" diameter x 1" length
   Wooden hub:
      (1) 1" diameter x ⅜" thick
   Round-head wood screw:
      (1) #4 x 1"
Permanent black marker,
   fine-point
Industrial-strength glue
Wood glue
Matte spray varnish
Needlenose pliers
Drill with ³/₃₂", ¹/₁₆",
   ⅛" & ⅜" drill bits

1. Transfer patterns, cut out shapes, and sand and seal wood for painting. Refer to General Instructions on page 6 for a list of supplies needed and for detailed information on preparing wood for painting.

2. Refer to General Instructions on pages 6-8 for detailed information on painting techniques that are used for this project.

3. Light buttermilk: Paint honey jar lid.

4. Taffy: Paint bees' wings and all four windmill wings on both sides.

5. Straw: Paint stripes on bear's dress in front and stripes and bow on dress in back. Paint bees' stripes.

6. Clay: Paint honey jar.

7. Black: Paint sleeves on bear's dress on both sides of both wood pieces. Paint stripes on bear's dress in front and in back. Paint bees' heads.

8. Chocolate: Paint bees' stripes.

9. Light cinnamon: Float-shade bees' stripes.

10. Mink: Paint bear's ears, head, paws, body, and feet on both sides.

**Designed by
Emily
Dinsdale**

11. Toffee: Paint bear's muzzle, tail, and palm of paw that shows. Lightly stipple tips of bear's paws, feet, ears, and around edges of bear's head and body on both sides.

12. Sable: Float-shade along bear's paws next to sleeves and across ankles on both sides. Float-shade under chin and across and inside ears. Wash 12" length of wooden dowel.

13. True ochre: Float-shade across gathers on honey jar lid and along bottoms of both bees. Float-shade across gathers on yoke and over straw-colored stripes on bear's dress. Float-shade bow on back of bear's dress.

14. Straw: Float-shade tips of windmill wings and bees' wings.

15. Black: Apply dots for buttons on front of bear's dress and apply dots for bear's eyes, nose, and mouth. Paint wooden dowel and hub for windmill assembly.

16. Country blue: Apply dots for irises in bear's eyes.

17. Light buttermilk: Paint around bear's irises. Paint lettering on honey jar using a #1 liner brush.

18. Black: Apply dots for pupils in bear's eyes.

19. Snow white: Apply dots in bear's eyes and on bear's nose. Apply dots for eyes on both bees and float-shade bees' wings. Stipple highlights on honey jar lid. Apply dots for lace trim around bear's neck on both sides and line trim around cuffs.

20. Chocolate: Float-shade inside bear's ears and line bear's eyebrows.

21. Line bear's eyelashes and the line that attaches the nose to the mouth with fine-point permanent black marker. Apply tiny dots on bear's muzzle and line around it. Line around honey jar and line gathers on jar lid. Line stitches on both sides of bear's dress and around lace trim. Line curls in bear's fur on both sides. Line around bees' wings. Line the antennae for the bee that will go on front of bear, positioned under bear's arm.

22. Finish with matte spray varnish because of linework.

23. Drill one $1/16$" hole in top of bear's head for placement of antennae. Drill one $1/8$" hole in bottom of one of bear's feet for placement of wooden dowel. Drill one $3/8$" hole through center back of bear's bodice for placement of wooden dowel for windmill assembly.

24. Using wood glue, glue arm holding honey jar to bear to cover drilled hole as shown in photograph on page 52. Glue one bee to front of bear, positioning so lined antennae looks natural. Glue remaining bee to back of bear. Glue wooden dowel inside hole in bottom of bear's foot.

25. Take both pieces of 19-gauge wire and curl for antennae. Using industrial-strength glue, glue one end of each antennae into drilled hole in top of bear's head. Position antennae as desired.

26. Assemble windmill. Refer to General Instructions on page 9 for detailed information and diagrams on assembling small windmills.

27. Using wood glue, glue windmill assembly into back of bear. Allow glue to dry thoroughly.

Windmill Wings
- Reproduce at 100%
- Cut 4
- Paint fronts & backs of windmill wings

Cat & Bird Windmill

Cat & Bird Windmill

Brushes:
Round fabric dye brush: #6
Flat brushes:
　#2, #4, #6, #8, #10, #12
Liner brush: #1

Acrylic Paint Colors:
Antique gold, black, brick red, buttermilk, Caucasian flesh, colonial blue, light blue, and yellow ochre

Supplies:
Pine for cat's body:
　$4^1/2$" wide x 8" high x $1/2$" thick
Plywood for windmill birds:
　8" wide x 3" high x $1/8$" thick
Wooden dowel:
　(1) $1/4$" diameter x 12" length
Windmill assembly:
　Wooden dowel:
　　(1) $3/8$" diameter x 1" length
　Wooden hub:
　　(1) 1" diameter x $3/8$" thick
　Round-head wood screw:
　　(1) #4 x 1"
Permanent black marker,
　fine-point
Wood glue
Matte spray varnish
Drill with $3/32$", $1/8$",
　$3/8$" & $1/4$" drill bits

1. Transfer patterns, cut out shapes, and sand and seal wood for painting. Refer to General Instructions on page 6 for a list of supplies needed and for detailed information on preparing wood for painting.

2. Refer to General Instructions on pages 6-8 for detailed information on painting techniques that are used for this project.

3. Yellow ochre: Paint cat. Paint 12" length of wooden dowel. Paint wooden dowel and hub for windmill assembly. Paint back side of cat and bird on cat's head.

4. Colonial blue: Paint all four windmill birds on both sides. Paint bird on cat's head.

5. Yellow ochre: Paint beaks on both sides of all four windmill birds. Paint bird's beak on cat's head.

6. Antique gold: Float-shade under and around cat's tail and under cat's chin. Wiggle all stripes on cat using a #1 liner brush.

7. Caucasian flesh: Dry-brush cat's cheeks and float-shade ear openings.

8. Brick red: Paint heart.

9. Light blue: Apply dots on all five birds on both sides.

10. Buttermilk: Paint cat's eyes.

11. Black: Apply dots for pupils in cat's eyes. Paint cat's nose.

12. Line cat's face with fine-point permanent black marker. Line cat and heart. Line birds and birds' eyes on both sides.

Designed by
Kathy
Distefano Griffiths

56

13. Finish with matte spray varnish because of linework.

14. Drill one ¼" hole in bottom of cat for placement of wooden dowel. Drill one ³/₈" hole through top of cat's tail for placement of wooden dowel for windmill assembly.

15. Assemble windmill. Refer to General Instructions on page 9 for detailed information and diagrams on assembling small windmills.

16. Using wood glue, glue wooden dowel inside hole in bottom of cat. Glue windmill assembly into front of cat. Allow glue to dry thoroughly.

Cat & Bird
• Reproduce at 100%
• Cut 1
  • Paint front & back of cat & bird — back side is not detail painted

Windmill Birds
  • Reproduce at 100%
  • Cut 4
  • Paint fronts & backs of windmill birds

Beehive Whirligig

Pictured on page 52.
Patterns on page 61.

Brushes:
Flat brushes: #2, #4, #6, #8
Liner brush: #1
Old toothbrush

Acrylic Paint Colors:
Charcoal grey, gold, iron oxide,
ivory, mocha, and yellow

Supplies:
Pine for beehive:
    4" wide x 4$\frac{1}{2}$" high x $\frac{1}{4}$" thick
Plywood for bee paddles:
    6" wide x 2" high x $\frac{1}{8}$" thick
Wooden dowel:
    (1) $\frac{1}{8}$" diameter x 12" length
Whirligig assembly:
    Wooden dowels:
        (1) $\frac{5}{16}$" diameter x 1$\frac{1}{2}$" length
        (2) $\frac{5}{16}$" diameter x 1" length
    Round-head wood screws:
        (2) #2 x $\frac{5}{8}$"
Permanent black marker,
    fine-point
Wood glue
Matte spray varnish
Drill with $\frac{3}{32}$", $\frac{1}{16}$",
    $\frac{5}{16}$" & $\frac{1}{8}$" drill bits

1. Transfer patterns, cut out shapes, and sand and seal wood for painting. Refer to General Instructions on page 6 for a list of supplies needed and for detailed information on preparing wood for painting.

2. Refer to General Instructions on pages 6-8 for detailed information on painting techniques that are used for this project.

3. Paint both sides of beehive and bee paddles identically.

4. Gold: Paint beehive. Paint 12" length of wooden dowel. Paint 1$\frac{1}{2}$" length of wooden dowel for whirligig assembly.

5. Mocha: Float-shade beehive. Lightly spatter beehive.

6. Iron oxide: Paint heart in center of beehive. Paint both 1" lengths of wooden dowels for whirligig assembly.

7. Yellow: Paint bees.

8. Charcoal grey: Paint bees' heads and stripes.

9. Ivory: Paint bees' wings. Paint plaid pattern on heart using a #1 liner brush and thinned paint.

10. Line beehive, heart, and bees with fine-point permanent black marker.

11. Finish with matte spray varnish because of linework.

12. Drill one $\frac{1}{8}$" hole in bottom of beehive for placement of wooden dowel. Drill one $\frac{5}{16}$" hole through beehive for placement of wooden dowel for whirligig assembly.

13. Place $\frac{5}{16}$" x 1$\frac{1}{2}$" wooden dowel through beehive and assemble whirligig. Refer to General Instructions on page 9 for detailed information and diagrams on assembling small whirligigs.

14. Using wood glue, glue wooden dowel inside hole in bottom of beehive. Place a small amount of wood glue into hole in beehive to secure whirligig assembly. Allow glue to dry thoroughly.

Designed by
Kathy
Distefano Griffiths

Watering Can Whirligig

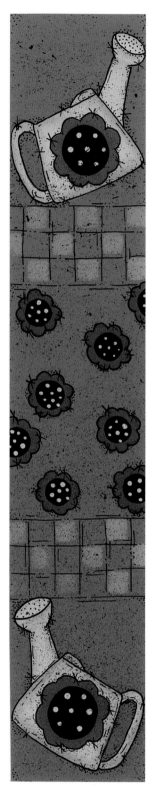

Watering Can Whirligig

Brushes:
Round fabric dye brush: #2
Round brushes: #2, #8
Flat brush: #6

Acrylic Paint Colors:
Antique white, black, country red, dark red, forest green, honey brown, mink, raw sienna, and true ochre

Supplies:
Pine for watering can:
   6" wide x 5" high x $\frac{1}{4}$" thick
Plywood for flower paddles:
   6" wide x 2" high x $\frac{1}{8}$" thick
Wooden dowel:
   (1) $\frac{1}{8}$" diameter x 12" length
Whirligig assembly:
   Wooden dowels:
     (1) $\frac{5}{16}$" diameter x 1$\frac{1}{2}$" length
     (2) $\frac{5}{16}$" diameter x 1" length
   Round-head wood screws:
     (2) #2 x $\frac{5}{8}$"
Permanent black marker,
   fine-point
Wood glue
Matte spray varnish
Drill with $\frac{3}{32}$", $\frac{1}{16}$",
   $\frac{5}{16}$" & $\frac{1}{8}$" drill bits

1. Transfer patterns, cut out shapes, and sand and seal wood for painting. Refer to General Instructions on page 6 for a list of supplies needed and for detailed information on preparing wood for painting.

2. Refer to General Instructions on pages 6-8 for detailed information on painting techniques that are used for this project.

3. Paint both sides of watering can and flowers identically.

4. Antique white: Paint watering can.

5. Honey brown: Paint bear's head and hands.

6. Country red: Paint bear's sleeves and flowers. Paint 12" length of wooden dowel.

7. Forest green: Paint watering can's handle and outside edge of watering spout. Paint wooden dowels for whirligig assembly.

8. Black: Paint area inside watering can's handle and paint watering spout. Paint flower centers. Paint bear's face. Apply dots for eyes.

9. Mink: Float-shade watering can.

10. Raw sienna: Float-shade bear's head.

11. Dark red: Float-shade bear's sleeves.

12. True ochre: Stipple small check border on bottom of watering can.

13. Honey brown: Mix with a little antique white. Lightly stipple bear's muzzle.

14. Antique white: Apply dots on sleeves, watering spout, and flower centers.

Designed by Jill Webster

15. Line watering can, bear's head and face, bear's sleeves, and flowers with fine-point permanent black marker.

16. Finish with matte spray varnish because of linework.

17. Drill one 1/8" hole in bottom of watering can for placement of wooden dowel. Drill one 5/16" hole through watering can for placement of wooden dowel for whirligig assembly.

18. Place 5/16" x 1 1/2" wooden dowel through watering can and assemble whirligig. Refer to General Instructions on page 9 for detailed information and diagrams on assembling small whirligigs.

19. Using wood glue, glue wooden dowel inside hole in bottom of watering can. Place a small amount of wood glue into hole in watering can to secure whirligig assembly. Allow glue to dry thoroughly.

Bear in Watering Can
• Reproduce at 100%
• Cut 1
• Paint front & back of bear & watering can

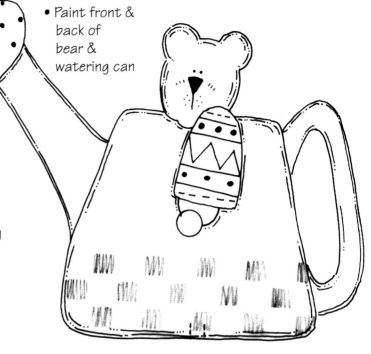

Beehive
• Instructions on page 58.
• Reproduce at 100%
• Cut 1
• Paint front & back of beehive

Flower Paddles
• Reproduce at 100%
• Cut 4
• Paint fronts & backs of flower paddles

Bee Paddles
• Instructions on page 58.
• Reproduce at 100%
• Cut 4
• Paint fronts & backs of bee paddles

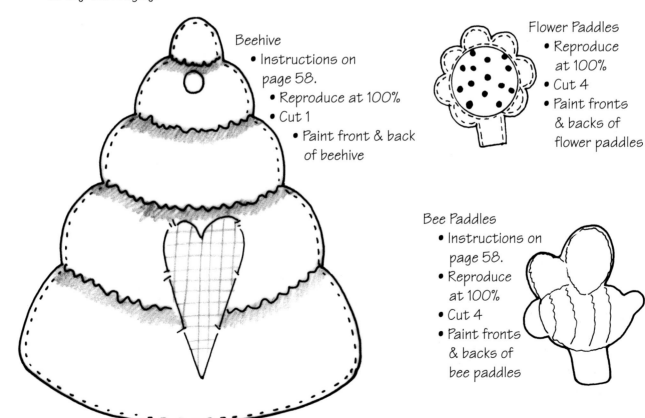

Rabbit on Rooster Whirligig

Brushes:
Round fabric dye brush: #4
Flat brushes: #2, #4, #8

Acrylic Paint Colors:
Antique rose, black, charcoal grey, coral, country red, honey brown, khaki tan, light avocado, light cinnamon, midnight blue, plum, terra cotta, toffee, and yellow

Supplies:
Pine for rabbit & rooster:
    5½" wide x 7" high x ½" thick
Plywood for paddles:
    6" wide x 3" high x ⅛" thick
Wooden dowel:
    (1) ¼" diameter x 12" length
Whirligig assembly:
    Wooden dowels:
        (1) ⅜" diameter x 2" length
        (2) ⅜" diameter x 1⅛" length
    Round-head wood screws:
        (2) #4 x 1"
    Washers: (2) ³⁄₁₆"
Permanent black marker,
    fine-point
Wood glue
Antique spray stain, golden oak
Matte spray varnish
Drill with ⁵⁄₆₄", ⅛", ⅜" & ¼" drill bits

1. Transfer patterns, cut out shapes, and sand and seal wood for painting. Refer to General Instructions on page 6 for a list of supplies needed and for detailed information on preparing wood for painting.

2. Refer to General Instructions on pages 6-8 for detailed information on painting techniques that are used for this project.

3. Paint both sides of rabbit and rooster identically.

4. Antique rose: Paint rooster's wattle and comb.

5. Light avocado: Paint rabbit's jacket and hat band.

6. Charcoal grey: Paint rabbit's hat and rooster's harness.

7. Midnight blue: Paint tail feathers.

8. Khaki tan: Paint rabbit's face, ears, and hands.

9. Plum: Paint cuffs on rabbit's jacket.

10. Honey brown: Paint rooster's beak.

11. Coral: Very lightly stipple rabbit's cheeks.

12. Toffee: Paint rooster's body.

13. Terra cotta: Lightly stipple rooster's eye area and outer edges of rooster's body.

14. Light cinnamon: Paint rabbit's boots.

15. Black: Apply dots for eyes on rabbit and rooster. Paint wooden dowels for whirligig assembly.

16. Country red: Paint all four paddles.

**Designed by
Debbie
Crabtree Lewis**

17. Yellow: Paint one star on each side of all four paddles. Apply dots for buttons on rabbit's jacket.

18. Lightly spray 12" length of wooden dowel and outer edges of rooster with antique spray stain.

19. Apply tiny dots on rooster with fine-point permanent black marker. Line around rooster's body, wattle, comb, and harness. Line around rabbit's hat band, face, ears, jacket, cuffs, hands, and boots. Line around stars on paddles.

20. Finish with matte spray varnish because of linework.

21. Drill one $1/4$" hole in bottom of rooster for placement of wooden dowel. Drill one $3/8$" hole through rooster for placement of wooden dowel for whirligig assembly.

22. Place $3/8$" x 2" wooden dowel through rooster and assemble whirligig. Refer to General Instructions on page 9 for detailed information and diagrams on assembling medium whirligigs.

23. Using wood glue, glue wooden dowel inside hole in bottom of rooster. Place a small amount of wood glue into hole in rooster to secure whirligig assembly. Allow glue to dry thoroughly.

Rabbit on Rooster
- Reproduce at 100%
- Cut 1
- Paint front & back of rabbit & rooster

Paddles
- Reproduce at 100%
- Cut 4
- Paint fronts & backs of paddles

64

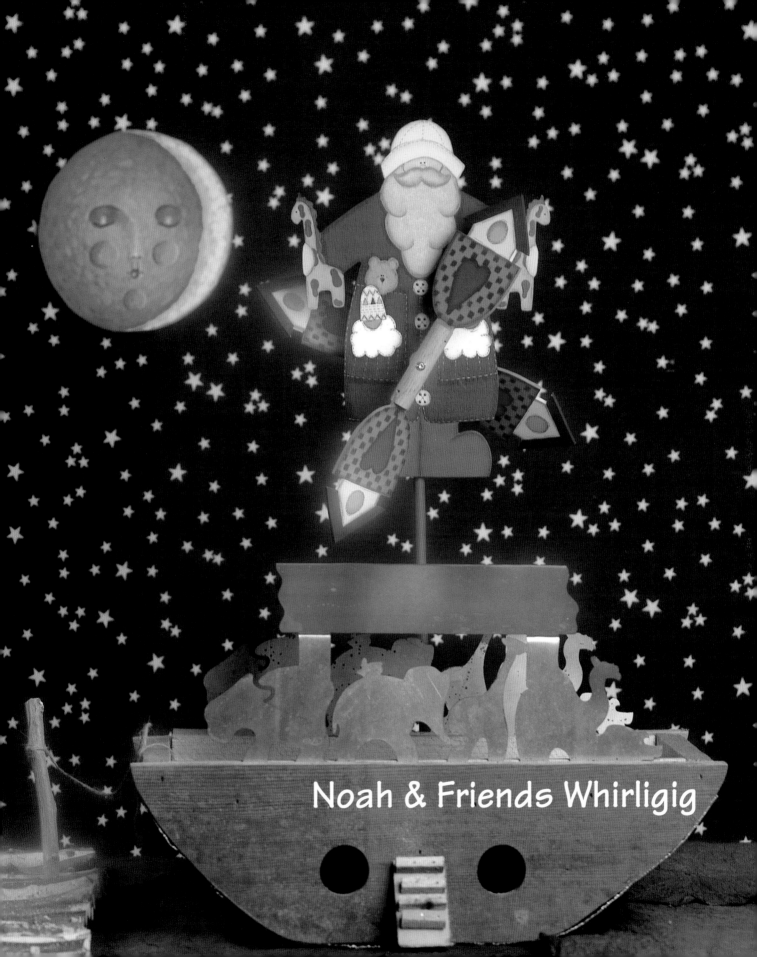

Noah & Friends Whirligig

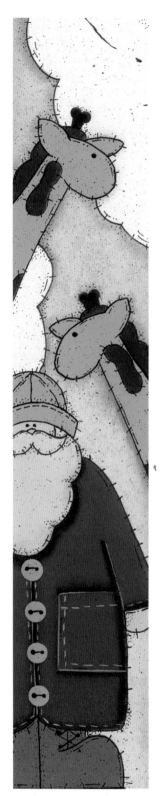

Noah & Friends Whirligig

Brushes:
Round fabric dye brush: #4
Round brushes: #2, #4, #6
Flat brushes: #6, #8
Liner brush: #6/0

Acrylic Paint Colors:
Antique gold, antique white, black, blue-grey, Caucasian flesh, country red, dark chocolate, dark red, grey, honey brown, midnight blue, raw sienna, sable, slate, snow white, true ochre, and yellow

Stencil Cream Colors:
Gooseberry and raspberry

Supplies:
Pine for Noah's body:
   9$^1/2$" wide x 12" high x $^3/4$" thick
Plywood for ark paddles:
   14" wide x 6" high x $^1/8$" thick
Wooden dowel:
   (1) $^3/8$" diameter x 16$^1/2$" length
Whirligig assembly:
   Wooden dowels:
      (1) $^3/4$" diameter x 3$^1/4$" length
      (2) $^3/4$" diameter x 2$^3/4$" length
   Round-head wood screws:
      (2) #7 x 1$^1/2$"
   Washers: (4) $^3/16$"
Stencil: $^1/4$" checks
Permanent black marker,
   fine-point
Wood glue
Antique spray stain, golden oak
Matte spray varnish
Drill with $^{11}/64$", $^1/8$",
   $^3/8$" & $^3/4$" drill bits

**Designed by
Jill
Webster**

1. Transfer patterns, cut out shapes, and sand and seal wood for painting. Refer to General Instructions on page 6 for a list of supplies needed and for detailed information on preparing wood for painting.

2. Refer to General Instructions on pages 6-8 for detailed information on painting techniques that are used for this project.

Noah & Giraffes:

3. Midnight blue: Paint Noah's raincoat on both sides.

4. Antique gold: Paint giraffes on both sides.

5. Grey: Paint Noah's beard and mustache. Paint Noah's hair on back side.

6. Caucasian flesh: Paint Noah's face. Paint Noah's hands on both sides.

7. Yellow: Paint Noah's hat on both sides.

8. Honey brown: Paint bears' faces and hands.

9. Snow white: Paint clouds on Noah's pockets.

10. Antique white: Paint bears' sleeves.

11. Country red: Paint Noah's boots on both sides. Paint 16$^1/2$" length of wooden dowel.

12. Dark chocolate: Paint manes on giraffes.

13. Dark red: Float-shade Noah's boots on both sides.

14. Black: Float-shade Noah's raincoat on both sides. Float-shade Noah's pockets.

15. Honey brown: Float-shade giraffes on both sides.

16. Raw sienna: Float-shade bears and Noah's face, nose, and hands.

17. Snow white: Float-shade bears' sleeves.

18. Slate: Stipple Noah's beard and mustache. Stipple Noah's hair on back side. Float-shade clouds on Noah's pockets.

19. Blue-grey: Float-shade Noah's beard and mustache.

20. True ochre: Float-shade Noah's hat on both sides.

21. Gooseberry: Stipple Noah's cheeks, then rub with a finger to blend.

22. Raspberry: Stipple bears' cheeks, then rub with a finger to blend.

23. Yellow: Paint buttons on Noah's raincoat.

24. True ochre: Paint designs on bears' sleeves. Float-shade buttons on Noah's raincoat. Paint the first and third rows of stitching on left bear's sleeve.

25. Midnight blue: Paint designs on bear's sleeve on Noah's left pocket.

26. Country red: Paint designs on bear's sleeve on Noah's right pocket. Paint the first, third, and fifth rows of stitching on right bear's sleeve. Paint the middle row of stitching on left bear's sleeve.

27. Midnight blue: Paint the second and fourth rows of stitching on right bear's sleeve.

28. Dark chocolate: Paint spots on giraffes on both sides.

29. Black: Apply dots for Noah's eyes, giraffes' eyes, and bears' eyes. Apply dots for buttons on Noah's raincoat. Paint giraffes' horns and bears' noses.

30. Antique white: Paint stitches on front and bottom edge of Noah's raincoat. Paint stitches on and around Noah's pockets.

31. Line around Noah's hat, face, beard, mustache, and hands with fine-point permanent black marker. Line around giraffes, bears, bears' sleeves, and clouds. Line around Noah's buttons and boots.

32. Finish with matte spray varnish because of linework.

Ark Paddles:

33. Paint both sides of ark paddles identically.

34. Sable: Paint bottoms of arks.

35. Antique white: Paint arks' cabins.

36. Midnight blue: Paint arks' roofs.

37. Antique gold: Paint windows on arks' cabins.

38. Chocolate: Float-shade edges of arks' cabins and bottoms of arks.

39. Dark chocolate: Stencil $1/4"$ checks on bottoms of arks.

40. Country red: Paint hearts on bottoms of arks.

41. Dark red: Float-shade hearts.

42. Honey brown: Float-shade the antique gold-colored circles.

43. Line around ark and hearts with fine-point permanent black marker.

44. Finish with matte spray varnish because of linework.

45. Lightly spray wooden dowels for whirligig assembly with antique spray stain.

46. Drill one ³/₈" hole in bottom of Noah's boots for placement of wooden dowel. Drill one ³/₄" hole through Noah for placement of wooden dowel for whirligig assembly.

47. Place ³/₄" x 3¹/₄" wooden dowel through Noah and assemble whirligig. Refer to General Instructions on page 9 for detailed information and diagrams on assembling large whirligigs.

48. Using wood glue, glue wooden dowel inside hole in bottom of Noah's boots. Place a small amount of wood glue into hole in Noah to secure whirligig assembly. Allow glue to dry thoroughly.

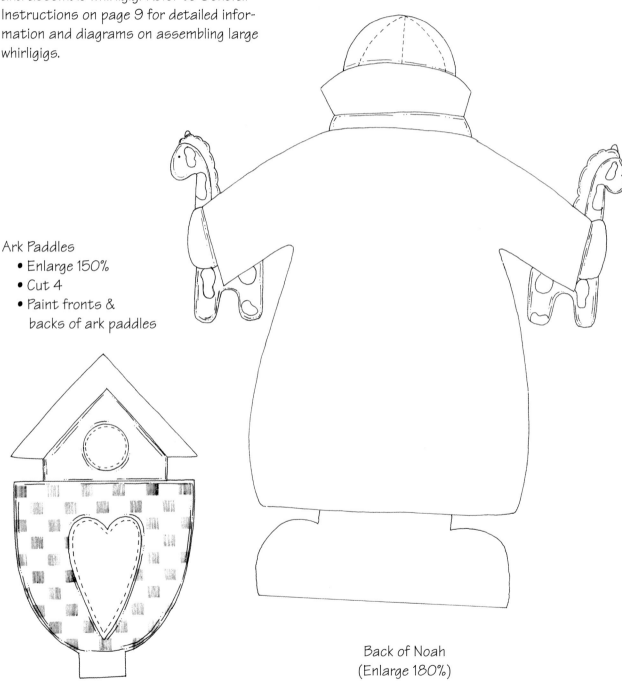

Ark Paddles
- Enlarge 150%
- Cut 4
- Paint fronts & backs of ark paddles

Back of Noah
(Enlarge 180%)

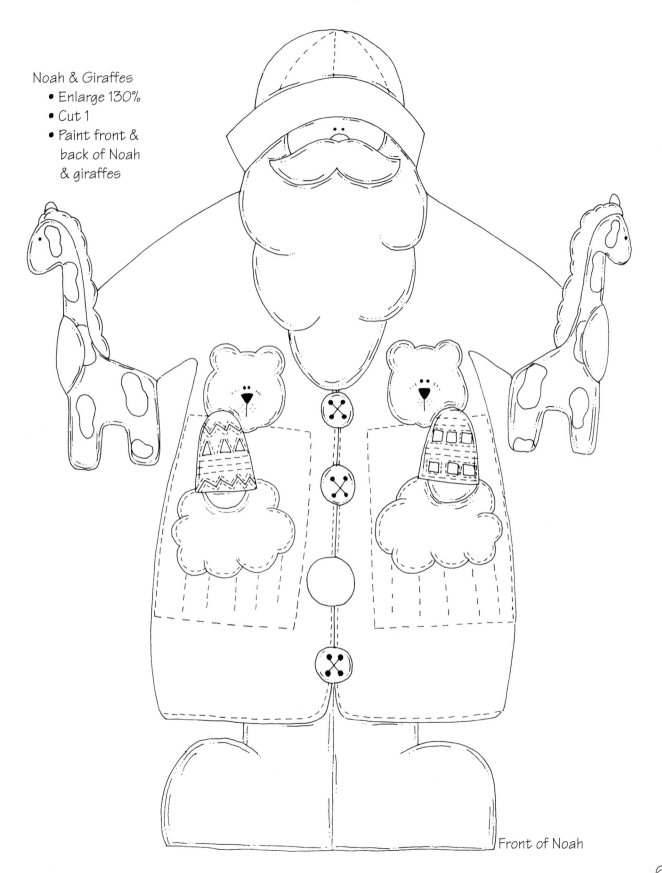

Noah & Giraffes
- Enlarge 130%
- Cut 1
- Paint front & back of Noah & giraffes

Front of Noah

69

Bunny & Carrots Whirligig

Brushes:
Round fabric dye brush: #3
Flat brushes: #2, #4, #6, #8, #12
Liner brush: #1

Acrylic Paint Colors:
Black, bright green, burnt orange, buttermilk, cashmere beige, Caucasian flesh, country blue, light green, medium green, mink, and true ochre

Supplies:
Pine for bunny's body:
  7" wide x 13" high x $^3/_4$" thick
Pine for bunny's arms:
  6" wide x 6" high x $^1/_4$" thick
Plywood for carrot paddles:
  10" wide x 6" high x
  $^1/_8$" thick
Wooden dowel:
  (1) $^3/_8$" diameter x
  16$^1/_2$" length
Whirligig assembly:
  Wooden dowels:
    (1) $^3/_4$" diameter
    x 3$^1/_4$" length
    (2) $^3/_4$" diameter
    x 2$^3/_4$" length
  Round-head
    wood screws:
    (2) #7 x 1$^1/_2$"
  Washers: (4) $^3/_{16}$"
Stencil: Dots
Permanent black marker,
  fine-point
Wood glue
Antique spray stain,
  golden oak
Matte spray varnish
Drill with $^{11}/_{64}$", $^1/_8$",
  $^3/_8$" & $^3/_4$" drill bits

Carrot Paddles
• Enlarge 140%
• Cut 4
• Paint fronts
  & backs of
  carrot paddles

Designed by
Kathy
Distefano Griffiths

1. Transfer patterns, cut out shapes, and sand and seal wood for painting. Refer to General Instructions on page 6 for a list of supplies needed and for detailed information on preparing wood for painting.

2. Refer to General Instructions on pages 6-8 for detailed information on painting techniques that are used for this project.

3. Paint both sides of bunny and carrot paddles identically.

4. Buttermilk: Paint bunny's head, arms, and legs. Paint 16$^1/_2$" length of wooden dowel. Paint wooden dowels for whirligig assembly.

5. Country blue: Paint bunny's dress.

6. Cashmere beige: Paint bunny's tail and the yoke and ruffle on bunny's dress.

7. True ochre: Paint flowers.

8. Burnt orange: Paint carrots.

9. Medium green: Paint carrot tops and leaves on flowers.

10. Caucasian flesh: Dry-brush bunny's cheeks and ear openings. Wash bunny's nose.

11. Cashmere beige: Float-shade bottom of bunny's ears above her head and above her foot.

12. Light green: Stipple highlights on carrot tops and on leaves on flowers.

13. Burnt orange: Wiggle all carrots on bunny's dress using a #1 liner brush. Line the trim on the neck of bunny's dress. Stipple in flower centers.

14. True ochre: Stipple dots on carrots, using dot stencil.

15. Bright green: Stroke carrot tops on the carrots on bunny's dress.

16. Mink: Apply dots on yoke and ruffle on bunny's dress.

17. Black: Apply dots for bunny's eyes.

18. Line around bunny's ears, head, face, body, legs, foot, tail, arms, dress, flowers, and carrots with fine-point permanent black marker.

19. Finish with matte spray varnish because of linework.

20. Lightly spray $16\frac{1}{2}$" length of wooden dowel with antique spray stain.

21. Using wood glue, glue bunny's arms to bunny as shown in photograph on page 70.

22. Drill one $\frac{3}{8}$" hole in bottom of bunny's feet for placement of wooden dowel. Drill one $\frac{3}{4}$" hole through bunny for placement of wooden dowel for whirligig assembly.

23. Place $\frac{3}{4}$" x $3\frac{1}{4}$" wooden dowel through bunny and assemble whirligig. Refer to General Instructions on page 9 for detailed information and diagrams on assembling large whirligigs.

24. Using wood glue, glue wooden dowel inside hole in bottom of bunny's feet. Place a small amount of wood glue into hole in bunny to secure whirligig assembly. Allow glue to dry thoroughly.

Bunny's Body & Bunny's Arms
- Enlarge 140%
- Cut 1 Bunny
- Cut 2 Arms
- Paint front & back of bunny's body
- Paint fronts & backs of bunny's arms — back sides are not detail painted

Fat Cat Wind Chime

Take the Time to Smell the Flowers!

Fat Cat Wind Chime

Brushes:
Round fabric dye brushes: #8, #10
Flat brushes: #2, #4, #8, #12
Liner brush: #2
Old toothbrush

Acrylic Paint Colors:
Buttermilk, charcoal grey, colonial blue, coral, honey brown, light green, straw, true ochre, and yellow ochre

Supplies:
Pine for fat cat sign:
  $10^1/_2$" wide x $9^1/_2$" high x $^3/_4$" thick
Pine for flowers & sun:
  8" wide x 3" high x $^1/_2$" thick
Wooden dowels:
  (1) $^1/_8$" diameter x 7" length
  (2) $^1/_8$" diameter x 4" length
  (6) $^1/_8$" diameter x 2" length
Scraps of green fabric
Linen jute: (1) 15" piece
Eye hook: (1) $^1/_4$"
Wind chime
Permanent black markers,
  fine-point & medium-point
Wood glue
Antique spray stain, golden oak
Matte spray varnish
Drill with $^1/_{16}$" & $^1/_8$" drill bits

1. Transfer patterns, cut out shapes, and sand and seal wood for painting. Refer to General Instructions on page 6 for a list of supplies needed and for detailed information on preparing wood for painting.

2. Refer to General Instructions on pages 6-8 for detailed information on painting techniques that are used for this project.

3. Paint both sides of wind chime identically.

4. Yellow ochre: Paint cat, including cat's tail.

5. Buttermilk: Paint sign. Stipple highlights on cat and spatter.

6. Colonial blue: Wash stripe around sign.

7. Honey brown: Float-shade and wash stripes (or wiggles) on cat.

8. Coral: Paint wood flowers. Paint flowers on front of cat's body. Stipple cat's cheeks. Mix with a little buttermilk and stipple highlights on all flowers.

9. Straw: Paint sun. Paint 7" long wooden dowel and all six 2" long wooden dowels. Paint a circle in each flower's center.

10. True ochre: Dry-brush all straw-colored dowels. Spatter sun.

11. Charcoal grey: Paint cat's eyes and nose.

12. Light green: Paint both 4" long wooden dowels. Paint stems and leaves on flowers on front of cat's body using a #2 liner brush.

**Designed by
Rebecca
Carter**

13. Line around cat's ears, face, body, feet and tail with fine-point permanent black marker. Line flowers and sign.

14. Line lettering on sign with medium-point permanent black marker.

15. Finish with matte spray varnish because of linework.

16. Carefully spray outer edges of sign with antique spray stain.

17. Drill one ¹/₁₆" hole in top of cat's head. Drill one ¹/₈" hole in top of sign to cat's left. Drill two ¹/₈" holes in top of sign to cat's right. Drill one ¹/₈" hole in bottom of each wood flower and in bottom of sun. Drill six ¹/₈" holes in top of sun, evenly spaced around arch.

18. Using wood glue, glue light green wooden dowels inside holes in top of sign as shown in photograph on page 73. Glue wood flowers to other ends of light green wooden dowels. Glue straw-colored 7" wooden dowel into hole in top of sign and glue sun to its other end. Glue straw-colored 2" wooden dowels into holes in arch on sun, varying their lengths. Allow glue to dry thoroughly.

19. Tie scraps of green fabric around wooden dowel stems for leaves.

20. Screw eye hook into drilled hole in top of cat's head. Thread linen jute through eye hook and tie a knot to form a loop for hanging.

21. Hang wind chime from cat's tail.

Sun & Flowers
• Reproduce at 100%
• Cut 1 Sun
• Cut 2 Flowers
• Paint fronts & backs of sun & flowers

Sun

Flower

Fat Cat Sign
• Enlarge 140%
• Cut 1
• Paint front & back of fat cat sign

Take the Time to Smell the Flowers!

Ark Wind Chime

Brushes:
Round fabric dye brush: #8
Round brush: #8
Flat brushes: #8, #20
Liner brush: #18/0

Acrylic Paint Colors:
Antique gold, antique white, black, blue-grey, burnt umber, country red, dark brown, dark green, dark red, forest green, honey brown, light cinnamon, medium green, midnight blue, mink, raw sienna, and true ochre

Supplies:
Pine for base & ark:
  13$\frac{1}{2}$" wide x 6$\frac{1}{2}$" high x $\frac{3}{4}$" thick
Pine for back board:
  3" wide x 12$\frac{1}{2}$" high x $\frac{3}{4}$" thick
Pine for giraffes:
  4$\frac{1}{2}$" wide x 9" high x $\frac{1}{2}$" thick
Pine for star & arrow:
  3" wide x 3" high x $\frac{1}{4}$" thick
Plywood for stars:
  4" wide x 4" high x $\frac{1}{8}$" thick
Plywood for sign:
  4" wide x 2" high x $\frac{1}{8}$" thick
Wooden wheels:
  (4) 1$\frac{1}{2}$" diameter with $\frac{1}{4}$" holes
Wooden dowels:
  (1) $\frac{1}{8}$" diameter x 2$\frac{1}{2}$" length
  (2) $\frac{1}{4}$" diameter x 2" length
Stencils: $\frac{1}{4}$" checks & $\frac{1}{2}$" checks
2-ply jute: (1) 18" piece
Wind chime
Permanent black marker,
  fine-point
Wood glue
Matte spray varnish
Drill with $\frac{1}{8}$", $\frac{1}{4}$" & $\frac{3}{4}$" drill bits

**Designed by
Jill
Webster**

1. Transfer patterns, cut out shapes, and sand and seal wood for painting. Refer to General Instructions on page 6 for a list of supplies needed and for detailed information on preparing wood for painting.

2. Refer to General Instructions on pages 6-8 for detailed information on painting techniques that are used for this project.

3. Forest green: Paint base on top and bottom. Paint back board and wooden disk on wind chime on both sides.

4. Medium green: Stencil $\frac{1}{2}$" checks on top of base and on front of back board.

5. Black: Paint $\frac{5}{8}$" checks on outside edges of base and back board.

6. Dark green: Float-shade $\frac{5}{8}$" black checks on right sides. Float-shade around top edge of base and back board.

7. Dark brown: Paint bottom of ark on both sides.

8. Light cinnamon: Stencil $\frac{1}{2}$" checks on bottom of ark on both sides.

9. Black: Float-shade edges on bottom of ark on both sides.

10. Antique white: Paint ark's cabin on both sides.

11. Mink: Float-shade edges on ark's cabin on both sides.

12. Country red: Paint ark's roof on both sides.

13. Dark red: Float-shade top edges of roof on both sides. Paint sign.

14. Antique gold: Paint all three stars, painting star for top of weathervane on both sides. Paint three windows on back of ark and two windows on front of ark as shown in patterns on page 79.

15. Honey brown: Paint a door on front of ark. Float-shade windows on both sides.

16. Raw sienna: Float-shade door.

17. Midnight blue: Paint arrow for weathervane on all sides and paint $2\frac{1}{2}$" length of wooden dowel.

18. Blue-grey: Paint all four wooden wheels and both 2" lengths of wooden dowels.

19. Country red: Stencil $\frac{1}{4}$" checks on sign.

20. Black: Paint lettering on sign using a #18/0 liner brush.

21. Antique white: Paint stitches around outside edges of bottom of ark on both sides. Paint lettering on sign.

22. True ochre: Paint giraffes on both sides.

23. Burnt umber: Paint manes on giraffes.

24. Dark brown: Float-shade outside edges of manes.

25. Black: Paint horns on giraffes.

26. Honey brown: Float-shade around all edges of giraffes.

27. Burnt umber: Apply dots on giraffes on both sides.

28. Black: Apply dots for eyes on both sides of both giraffes.

29. Line around base, back board, ark, windows, door, sign, and both giraffes with fine-point permanent black marker. Line lettering over the door.

30. Finish with matte spray varnish because of linework.

31. Drill one $\frac{1}{8}$" hole in top of ark. Drill one $\frac{1}{8}$" hole in bottom of $\frac{1}{4}$"-thick star. Drill one $\frac{1}{8}$" hole through the center of the arrow. Drill two $\frac{1}{4}$" holes through bottom of ark for placement of wooden dowels for wheels. Drill one $\frac{3}{4}$" hole at top of back board.

32. Attach small giraffe to the wind chime by replacing the center ornament.

33. Using wood glue, glue $\frac{1}{4}$" wooden dowels inside holes in bottom of ark. Glue wooden wheels onto the wooden dowels. Place $\frac{1}{8}$" wooden dowel through the arrow and place a little glue in the middle to secure it. Glue one end of this dowel into hole in bottom of $\frac{1}{4}$"-thick star and the other end into hole in top of ark. Glue the bottom of all four wooden wheels to the base as shown in photograph. Glue one $\frac{1}{8}$"-thick star to each side of ark and glue sign centered above three windows on back of ark. Glue back board inside indentation on base so the bottoms are flush. Glue large giraffe to base as shown in photograph. Allow glue to dry thoroughly.

34. Forest green: Paint inside drilled hole at top of back board.

35. Blue-grey: Touch-up paint on wooden dowels and wooden wheels.

36. Using wood glue, glue wooden disk on wind chime to center bottom of base. Allow glue to dry thoroughly.

37. Thread 2-ply jute through drilled hole in top of back board and tie a knot to form a loop for hanging.

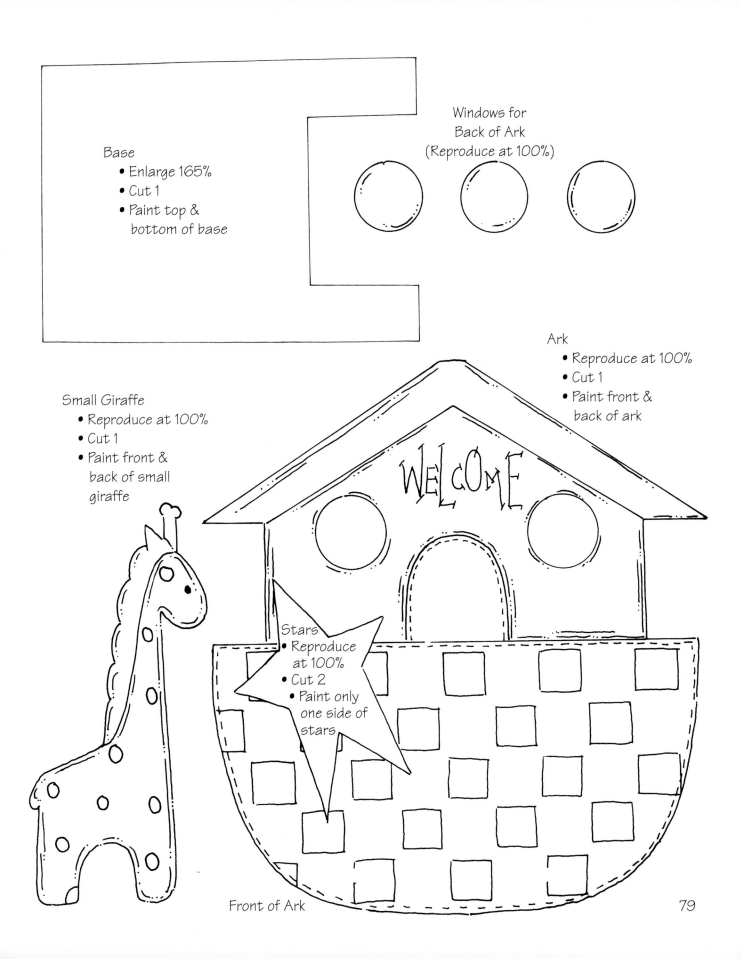

Base
- Enlarge 165%
- Cut 1
- Paint top & bottom of base

Windows for Back of Ark
(Reproduce at 100%)

Ark
- Reproduce at 100%
- Cut 1
- Paint front & back of ark

Small Giraffe
- Reproduce at 100%
- Cut 1
- Paint front & back of small giraffe

WELCOME

Stars
- Reproduce at 100%
- Cut 2
- Paint only one side of stars

Front of Ark

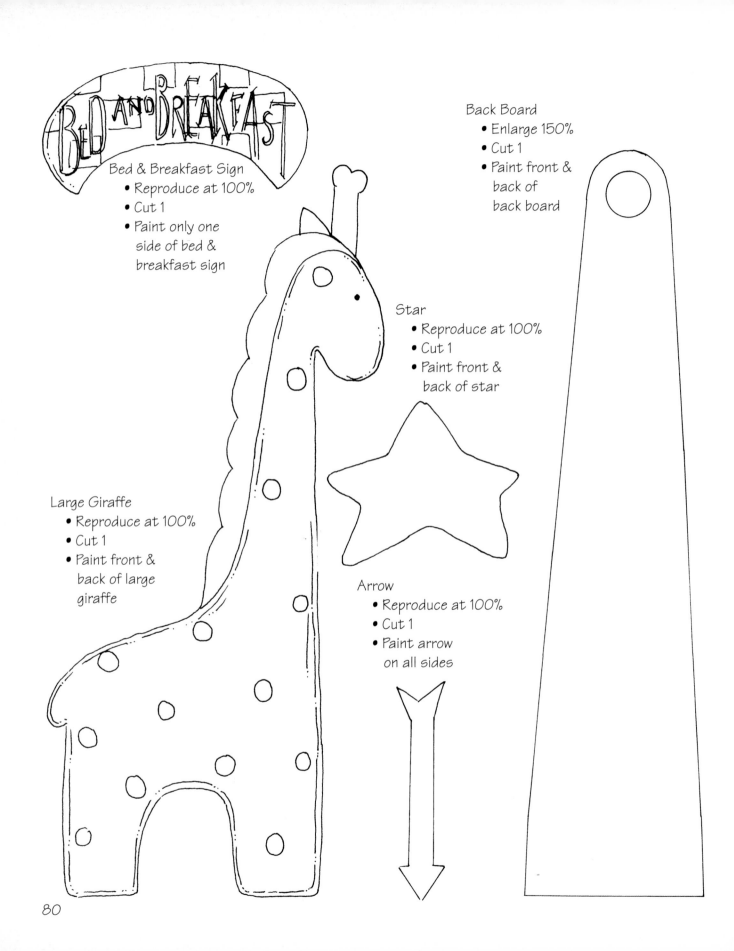

Bed & Breakfast Sign
- Reproduce at 100%
- Cut 1
- Paint only one side of bed & breakfast sign

Back Board
- Enlarge 150%
- Cut 1
- Paint front & back of back board

Star
- Reproduce at 100%
- Cut 1
- Paint front & back of star

Large Giraffe
- Reproduce at 100%
- Cut 1
- Paint front & back of large giraffe

Arrow
- Reproduce at 100%
- Cut 1
- Paint arrow on all sides

Every Bunny Loves A Garden
Wind Chime

Every Bunny Loves A Garden Wind Chime

Brushes:
Flat brushes: #4, #6
Liner brushes: #1, #2

Acrylic Paint Colors:
Black, blue-grey, bright orange, bright red, charcoal grey, driftwood, dusty rose, light buttermilk, light green, medium green, olive green, pumpkin, tangerine, and tomato red

Supplies:
Pine for bunny sign, tomato & carrot:
   6" wide x 10" high x $^3/_4$" thick
Pine for pea pods:
   2$^1/_2$" wide x 3" high x $^1/_2$" thick
Wooden half eggs: (2) $^3/_4$"
Wooden primitive star:
   (1) $^1/_2$" wide x $^1/_8$" thick
Wooden hole plugs: (3) $^3/_8$"
18-gauge wire, green: (2) 6" pieces
Linen jute: (1) 18" piece
Eye hooks: (5) $^1/_4$"
Wind chime
Permanent black marker,
   fine-point
Wood glue
Matte spray varnish
Needlenose pliers
Drill with $^1/_{16}$" & $^3/_8$" drill bits

1. Transfer patterns, cut out shapes, and sand and seal wood for painting. Refer to General Instructions on page 6 for a list of supplies needed and for detailed information on preparing wood for painting.

2. Refer to General Instructions on pages 6-8 for detailed information on painting techniques that are used for this project.

3. Paint both sides of wind chime identically.

4. Light buttermilk: Paint bunny.

5. Blue-grey: Paint sign.

6. Tangerine: Paint carrot.

7. Light green: Paint carrot top, pea pods, and wooden primitive star for tomato stem.

8. Bright red: Paint tomato.

9. Bright orange: Paint wooden half eggs for ladybugs and float-shade around carrot.

10. Medium green: Float-shade carrot top, pea pods, and tomato stem. Paint wooden hole plugs for peas.

11. Tomato red: Float-shade tomato.

12. Olive green: Stipple highlights on carrot top and line the curl on tomato stem.

13. Pumpkin: Float-shade around carrot.

14. Driftwood: Float-shade around bunny.

15. Dusty rose: Stipple bunny's cheeks, nose, and ear openings.

Designed by
Emily
Dinsdale

16. Sand edges of sign until unpainted wood is showing through.

17. Light buttermilk: Paint lettering on sign using a #2 liner brush.

18. Black: Paint ladybug's heads and spots.

19. Charcoal grey: Spatter all wood pieces.

20. Line bunny's eye and antennae for ladybugs with fine-point permanent black marker.

21. Finish with matte spray varnish because of linework.

22. Drill one $\frac{1}{16}$" hole in top of bunny's ears. Drill one $\frac{1}{16}$" hole in top of carrot. Drill three $\frac{1}{16}$" holes on bottom of sign, evenly spaced from side to side.

23. Screw eye hooks into drilled holes.

24. Drill one $\frac{1}{16}$" hole through top of each pea pod. Drill one $\frac{1}{16}$" hole in top of tomato. Drill three $\frac{3}{8}$" holes $\frac{1}{16}$" deep on front of one pea pod, evenly spaced in center.

25. Using wood glue, glue peas into $\frac{1}{16}$" deep holes on pea pod. Glue tomato stem to top of one side of tomato. Glue ladybugs into position on sign. Allow glue to dry thoroughly.

26. Take one piece of 18-gauge wire and curl one end. Thread it through hole in top of one pea pod, then curl again. Continue threading it through eye hook on left side of sign and curl again. Finally, thread it through hole in top of other pea pod and curl wire. Take remaining piece of 18-gauge wire and glue it into drilled hole in top of tomato. Allow glue to dry thoroughly. Curl wire slightly and thread it through the eye hook on right side of sign. Curl again.

27. Use eye hook on top of carrot to attach it to the wind chime by replacing the center ornament. Attach wind chime ring to eye hook in center of sign.

28. Thread linen jute through eye hook in top of bunny's ears and tie a knot to form a loop for hanging.

Bunny Sign
• Enlarge 130%
• Cut 1
• Paint front & back of bunny sign

Every Bunny Loves A Garden

Tomato
• Enlarge 130%
• Cut 1
• Paint front & back of tomato

Carrot
• Enlarge 130%
• Cut 1
• Paint front & back of carrot

Pea Pods
• Enlarge 130%
• Cut 1 from each pattern
• Paint fronts & backs of pea pods

Rooster Weathervane

Brushes:
Round fabric dye brush: #8
Flat brushes: #10, #12
Liner brush: #1
Old toothbrush

Acrylic Paint Colors:
Brick red, dark green, true ochre, and yellow ochre

Supplies:
Pine for rooster's body:
    $8^1/2$" wide x $7^1/2$" high x $3/4$" thick
Plywood for rooster's wings (hearts):
    3" wide x 3" high x $1/8$" thick
Pine for arrow:
    13" wide x 2" high x $3/4$" thick
Wooden dowel:
    (1) $3/8$" diameter x $7^1/2$" length
Wooden block: (1) $3^1/4$" square
Stencils: $1/2$" checks & $1/2$" hearts
Cellophane tape: $3/4$"-wide
Raffia
Permanent black marker,
    fine-point
Wood glue
Antiquing medium
Clean cloth
Matte spray varnish
Hammer
Phillips screwdriver
Drill with $3/8$" drill bit

1. Transfer patterns, cut out shapes, and sand and seal wood for painting. Refer to General Instructions on page 6 for a list of supplies needed and for detailed information on preparing wood for painting.

2. Refer to General Instructions on pages 6-8 for detailed information on painting techniques that are used for this project.

3. Paint both sides of weathervane identically.

4. Yellow ochre: Paint wooden block on all sides and paint rooster's head and body.

5. Dark green: Mask off top and bottom of wooden block on all four sides with $3/4$"-wide cellophane tape. Stipple $1/2$" checks around center of wooden block on all four sides. Remove tape. Stipple $1/2$" checks on rooster's body. Paint arrow on all sides and paint wooden dowel. Lightly spatter wooden block and rooster's head and body.

6. True ochre: Paint rooster's beak.

7. Brick red: Paint rooster's wattle, comb, and tail feathers. Paint hearts for rooster's wings. Stipple $1/2$" hearts around top and bottom of wooden block on all four sides.

8. Line around rooster and around wooden block with fine-point permanent black marker.

9. Sand edges of all wood pieces. Make rooster's eyes and random marks on rooster's tail feathers using a hammer and a Phillips screwdriver.

Designed by
Kathy
Distefano Griffiths

10. Finish with matte spray varnish because of linework.

11. Antique by applying antiquing medium to all wood pieces, making sure it gets deep into crevices made by the Phillips screwdriver. Wipe off excess with a clean cloth.

12. Drill one ³/₈" hole in top center of wooden block. Drill one ³/₈" hole in bottom of rooster. Drill one ³/₈" hole through center of arrow.

13. Using wood glue, glue wooden dowel into hole in top of wooden block. Place wooden dowel through drilled hole in arrow and place a little glue in the middle to secure it. Glue top end of dowel into hole in bottom of rooster. Glue heart wings on rooster's body as shown in photograph on page 84. Allow glue to dry thoroughly.

14. Tie a raffia bow around the wooden dowel just above the wooden block.

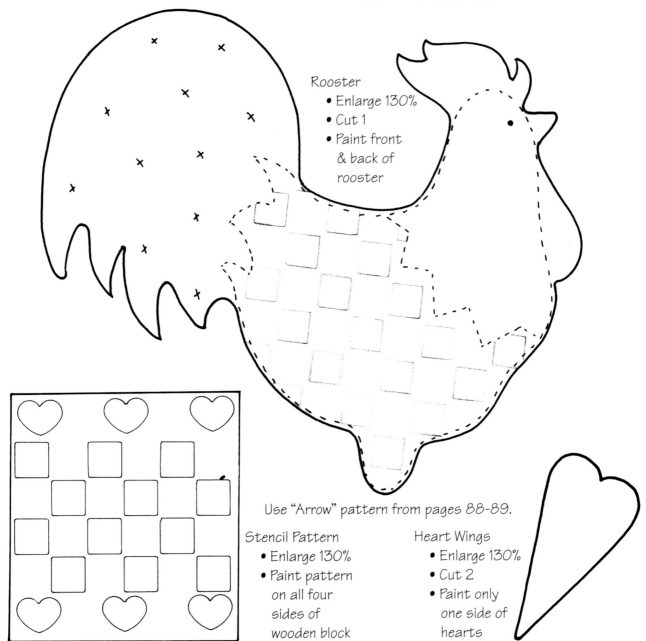

Rooster
- Enlarge 130%
- Cut 1
- Paint front & back of rooster

Use "Arrow" pattern from pages 88-89.

Stencil Pattern
- Enlarge 130%
- Paint pattern on all four sides of wooden block

Heart Wings
- Enlarge 130%
- Cut 2
- Paint only one side of hearts

Dove Weathervane

Dove Weathervane

Brushes:
Flat brushes: #6, #8
Old toothbrush

Acrylic Paint Colors:
Black, charcoal grey, evergreen, khaki tan, light buttermilk, and tomato red

Supplies:
Pine for dove's body:
  10$\frac{1}{2}$" wide x 5$\frac{1}{2}$" high x $\frac{3}{4}$" thick
Pine for dove's wings:
  6" wide x 7" high x $\frac{3}{8}$" thick
Pine for arrow:
  13" wide x 2" high x $\frac{3}{4}$" thick
Plywood for hearts:
  8" wide x 2$\frac{1}{2}$" high x $\frac{1}{8}$" thick
Wooden stick: (1) Approximately
  $\frac{3}{8}$" diameter x 11" length
Wooden block: (1) 3$\frac{1}{4}$" square
Wooden apples: (2) 1" diameter
Waxed ivy sprays
Twigs
Tiny silk leaf
Wood glue
Antique spray stain, golden oak
Matte spray varnish
Hammer
Carpet tacks: (4) $\frac{3}{4}$"
Wood carving tool
Drill with $\frac{3}{8}$" drill bit

1. Transfer patterns, cut out shapes, and sand and seal wood for painting. Refer to General Instructions on page 6 for a list of supplies needed and for detailed information on preparing wood for painting.

2. Refer to General Instructions on pages 6-8 for detailed information on painting techniques that are used for this project.

3. Paint both sides of weathervane identically.

4. Carve out a few grooves along top edges of arrow and wooden block using a wood carving tool.

5. Lightly spray arrow and wooden block with antique spray stain.

6. Light buttermilk: Paint dove's body and dove's wings.

7. Khaki tan: Paint dove's beak.

8. Tomato red: Paint arrow on all sides. Paint all four hearts and both wooden apples for cherries.

9. Evergreen: Paint wooden block on all sides.

Arrow
• Reproduce at 100%
• Cut 1
• Paint arrow on all sides

**Designed by
Emily
Dinsdale**

10. Lightly sand edges of all wood pieces.

11. Charcoal grey: Spatter all wood pieces.

12. Black: Apply dots for dove's eyes.

13. Tack hearts to centers of wooden block sides with carpet tacks.

14. Light buttermilk: Lightly spatter wooden block.

15. Drill one $^3/_8$" hole in top center of wooden block. Drill one $^3/_8$" hole in bottom of dove. Drill one $^3/_8$" hole through center of arrow. These holes must be large enough to accommodate the wooden stick.

16. Using wood glue, glue wooden stick into hole in top of wooden block. Place wooden stick through drilled hole in arrow and place a little glue in the middle to secure it. Glue top end of stick into hole in bottom of dove. Glue wings on dove's body as shown in photograph on page 87. Allow glue to dry thoroughly.

17. Glue cherries to twigs for cherry stems then glue them into dove's mouth. Glue a tiny silk leaf to cherry stem.

18. Lightly spray outer edges of dove with antique spray stain. Spray remaining wood pieces.

19. Wrap waxed ivy sprays around wooden stick.

20. Finish with matte spray varnish.

Hearts
- Enlarge 140%
- Cut 4
- Paint only one side of hearts

Dove's Body & Dove's Wings
- Enlarge 140%
- Cut 1 Dove
- Cut 2 Wings
- Paint fronts & backs of dove's body & dove's wings

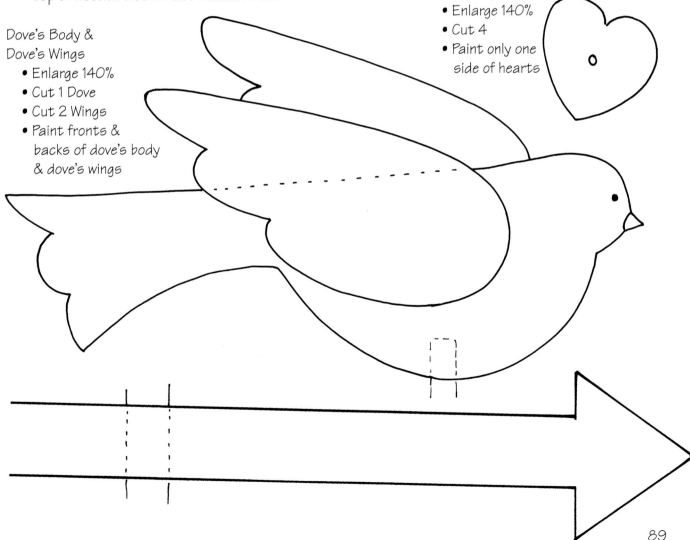

89

S.S. Ark Weathervane

**Designed by
Jill
Webster**

Brushes:
Round fabric dye brush: #8
Round brushes: #4, #8
Flat brushes: #4, #8, #12
Liner brush: #1
Old toothbrush

Acrylic Paint Colors:
Antique white, black, blue-grey, chocolate, country red, dark blue, honey brown, khaki tan, maroon, midnight blue, mink, sable, and true ochre

Supplies:
Pine for ark:
  7$^{1}/_{2}$" wide x 7$^{1}/_{2}$" high x $^{3}/_{4}$" thick
Plywood for hearts, stars & sign:
  12" wide x 5$^{1}/_{2}$" high x $^{1}/_{8}$" thick
Pine for arrow:
  13" wide x 2" high x $^{3}/_{4}$" thick
Wooden dowel:
  (1) $^{3}/_{8}$" diameter x 9$^{1}/_{2}$" length
Wooden block: (1) 3$^{1}/_{4}$" square
Wooden wheels:
  (1) 1$^{1}/_{2}$" diameter with $^{3}/_{8}$" hole
  (1) 1$^{3}/_{4}$" diameter with $^{3}/_{8}$" hole
  (1) 2$^{1}/_{4}$" diameter with $^{3}/_{8}$" hole
Stencil: $^{1}/_{2}$" checks
Permanent black marker,
  fine-point
Wood glue
Matte spray varnish
Drill with $^{3}/_{8}$" drill bit

1. Transfer patterns, cut out shapes, and sand and seal wood for painting. Refer to General Instructions on page 6 for a list of supplies needed and for detailed information on preparing wood for painting.

2. Refer to General Instructions on pages 6-8 for detailed information on painting techniques that are used for this project.

3. Sable: Paint bottom of ark on both sides.

4. Chocolate: Stencil $^{1}/_{2}$" checks and float-shade edges on bottom of ark on both sides.

5. Antique white: Paint ark's cabin on both sides.

6. Mink: Float-shade edges of ark's cabin on both sides.

7. Midnight blue: Paint ark's roof on top and on both sides. Paint arrow on all sides and paint 2$^{1}/_{4}$" wooden wheel.

8. Black: Float-shade top edges of ark's roof and arrow on all sides.

9. True ochre: Paint five windows on back of ark and two windows on front of ark as shown in patterns on page 93. Paint both stars.

10. Blue-grey: Paint wooden block on all sides and paint 1$^{1}/_{2}$" wooden wheel. Paint doors on front of ark.

11. Honey brown: Float-shade windows on both sides.

12. Midnight blue: Float-shade doors and apply dots for door handles.

13. Country red: Paint all three hearts, painting heart for front of ark on both sides.

14. Khaki tan: Paint sign. Paint center squares on wooden block on all four sides.

15. Sable: Float-shade sign and edges of center squares. Spatter ark on both sides.

16. Chocolate: Spatter ark on both sides.

17. Dark blue: Paint $1^3/4$" wooden wheel. Float-shade edges of wooden block and around center of $1^1/2$" wooden wheel.

18. Khaki tan: Spatter wooden block.

19. Maroon: Paint wooden dowel.

20. Antique white: Paint stitches on both sides of ark's roof and arrow.

21. Midnight blue: Float-shade around center of $1^3/4$" wooden wheel.

22. Black: Float-shade around center of $2^1/4$" wooden wheel. Paint lettering on sign using a #1 liner brush.

23. Sand edges of hearts and stars.

24. Line around center squares, ark, windows, doors, and sign with fine-point permanent black marker. Line the words "S.S. ARK" on front of ark as shown in photograph on page 90.

25. Finish with matte spray varnish because of linework.

26. Drill one $3/8$" hole in top center of wooden block. Drill one $3/8$" hole in bottom of ark. Drill one $3/8$" hole through center of arrow.

27. Using wood glue, glue wooden dowel into hole in top of wooden block. Place wooden dowel through the three wooden wheels, then through the arrow, and place a little glue in the middle to secure it. Glue top end of dowel into hole in bottom of ark. Glue large heart and sign on front of ark as shown in photograph. Glue hearts and stars, alternately, on center squares on wooden block. Allow glue to dry thoroughly.

Hearts & Stars
• Reproduce at 100%
• Cut 2 Hearts
• Cut 2 Stars
• Paint only one side of hearts & stars

Center Square Pattern
• Reproduce at 100%
• Paint pattern on all four sides of wooden block

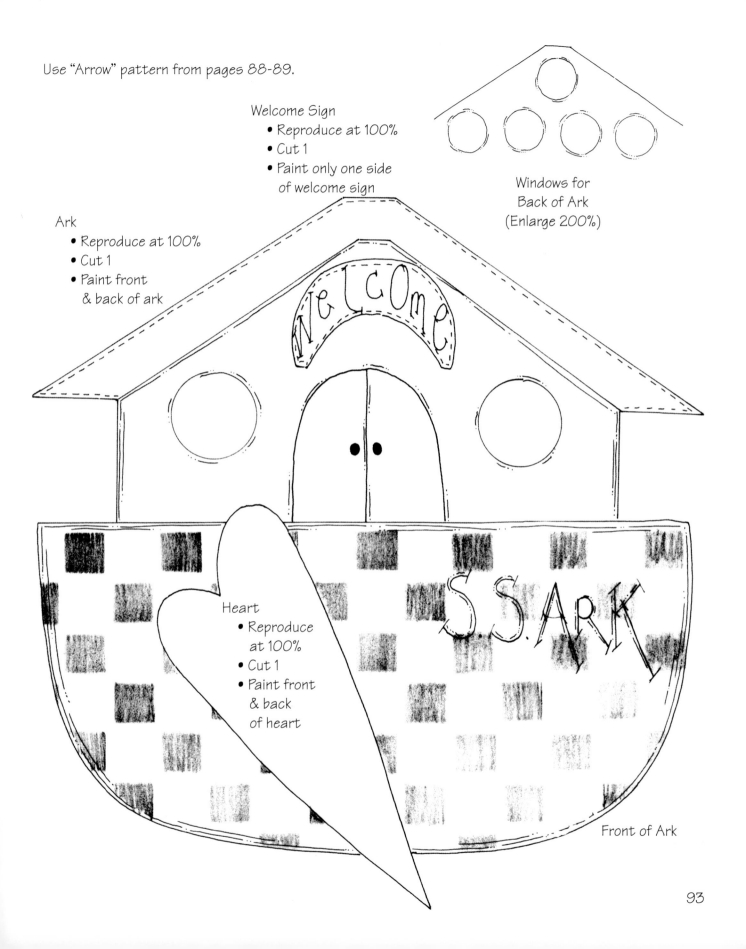

Use "Arrow" pattern from pages 88-89.

Welcome Sign
- Reproduce at 100%
- Cut 1
- Paint only one side
  of welcome sign

Windows for
Back of Ark
(Enlarge 200%)

Ark
- Reproduce at 100%
- Cut 1
- Paint front
  & back of ark

Welcome

S.S. Ark

Heart
- Reproduce
  at 100%
- Cut 1
- Paint front
  & back
  of heart

Front of Ark

93

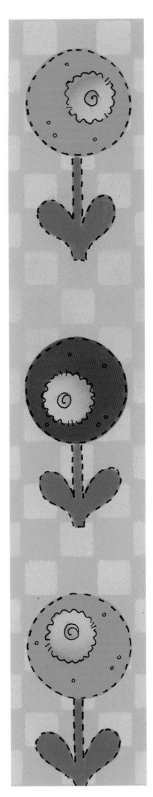

Designed by
Kathy
Distefano Griffiths

To The Garden Sign

Brushes:
Round fabric dye brush: #10
Flat brushes: #2, #4, #6, #8,
    #10, #12, #14, #16
Old toothbrush

Acrylic Paint Colors:
Brick red, buttermilk, Caucasian
flesh, colonial blue, dark colonial
blue, honey brown, medium green,
and yellow ochre

Supplies:
Pine for top section of sign:
    11" wide x 6" high x $\frac{3}{4}$" thick
Pine for bottom section of sign:
    13" wide x 4" high x $\frac{3}{4}$" thick
Pine for bird:
    4" wide x $3\frac{1}{2}$" high x $\frac{3}{8}$" thick
Pine for bird's wing (heart):
    2" wide x $1\frac{1}{4}$" high x $\frac{1}{4}$" thick
19-gauge wire, black: (3) 5" pieces
Eye hooks: (4) $\frac{1}{4}$"
Stencil: $\frac{3}{8}$" checks
Sawtooth hanger
Permanent black marker,
    fine-point
Industrial-strength glue
Wood glue
Matte spray varnish
Hammer
Nails: (2) $\frac{1}{2}$"
Needlenose pliers
Drill with $\frac{1}{16}$" drill bit

1. Transfer patterns, cut out
    shapes, and sand and seal
    wood for painting. Refer to
    General Instructions on
    page 6 for a list of supplies

needed and for detailed
information on preparing
wood for painting.

2. Refer to General Instructions
    on pages 6-8 for detailed
    information on painting tech-
    niques that are used for this
    project.

3. Colonial blue: Paint bird and top
    section of sign.

4. Colonial blue: Mix with a little
    buttermilk. Paint bottom section
    of sign. Stipple $\frac{3}{8}$" checks on
    bird and on top section of sign.

5. Colonial blue: Stipple $\frac{3}{8}$" checks
    on bottom section of sign.

6. Dark colonial blue: Spatter bird
    and top and bottom sections
    of sign.

7. Caucasian flesh: Paint large
    flower center.

8. Brick red: Paint two flowers.

9. Dark colonial blue: Paint remain-
    ing two flowers and paint heart
    for bird's wing. Apply dot for
    bird's eye.

10. Colonial blue: Paint back sides of
    top and bottom sections of sign
    and bird.

11. Medium green: Paint stems and
    leaves on flowers.

12. Brick red: Paint lettering using a
    #2 flat brush.

13. Yellow ochre: Paint flower
    centers.

14. Honey brown: Float-shade ³/₄ of the way around flower centers. Float-shade a small "C" in the middle of each flower center. Paint bird's beak.

15. Line stitches and details on top and bottom sections of sign and on bird with fine-point permanent black marker.

16. Finish with matte spray varnish because of linework.

17. Using wood glue, glue heart to bird for wing as shown in photograph on page 94.

18. Drill one ¹/₁₆" hole in bottom of bird. Drill one ¹/₁₆" hole in the top of top section of sign. Drill two ¹/₁₆" holes in bottom of top section of sign, 1¹/₂" from each side. Drill two ¹/₁₆" holes in the top of bottom section of sign, 2" from each side.

19. Screw eye hooks into drilled holes in top and bottom sections of sign.

20. Thread one 5" piece of 19-gauge wire through eye hooks on left side of sign and curl ends to secure top section of sign to bottom section of sign. Cut off excess wire. Repeat on right side.

21. Curl one 5" piece of 19-gauge wire and, using industrial-strength glue, glue one end inside hole in bottom of bird and other end inside hole in top of top section of sign.

22. Nail a sawtooth hanger onto back of top section of sign for hanging.

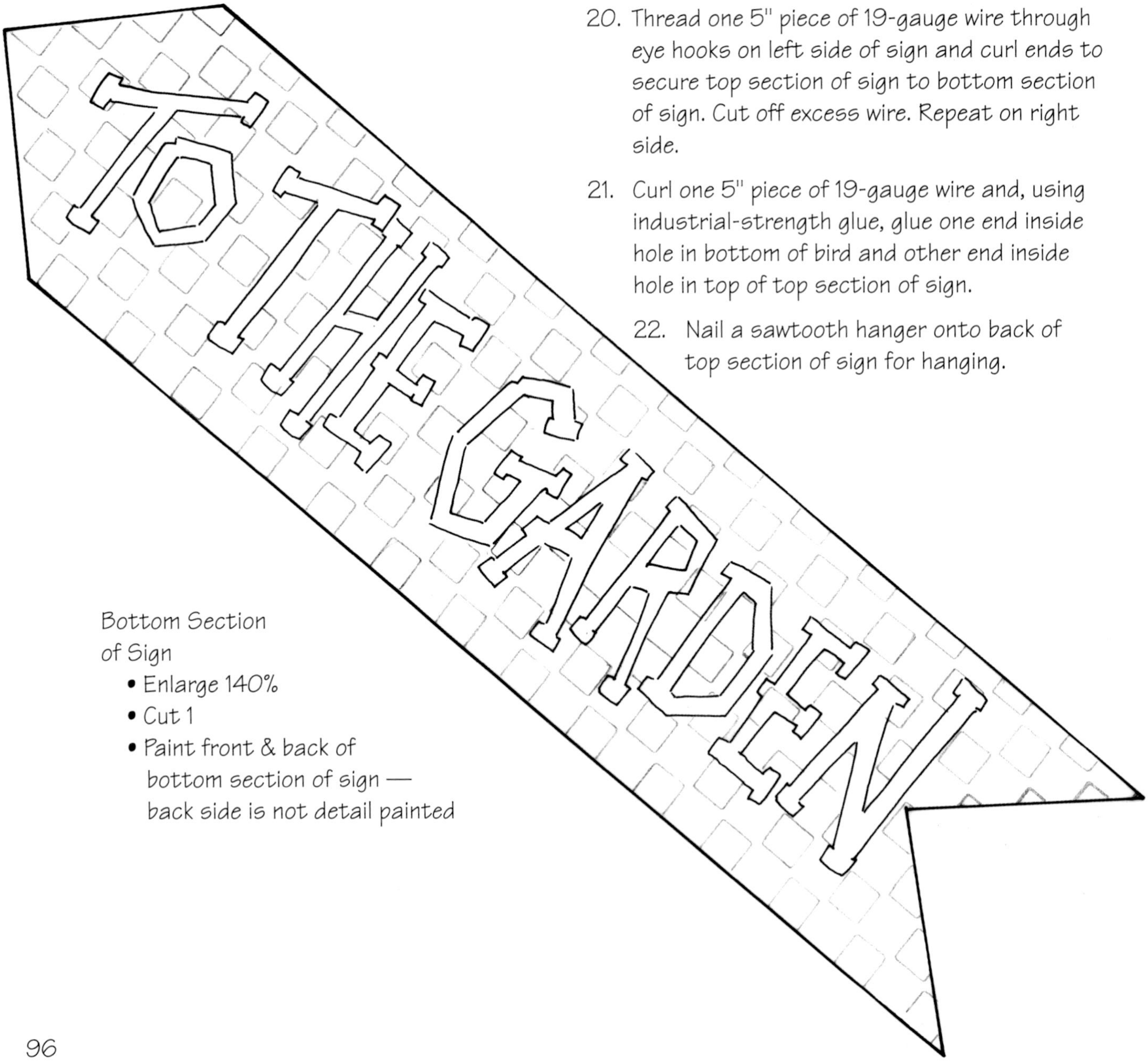

Bottom Section
of Sign
- Enlarge 140%
- Cut 1
- Paint front & back of
  bottom section of sign —
  back side is not detail painted

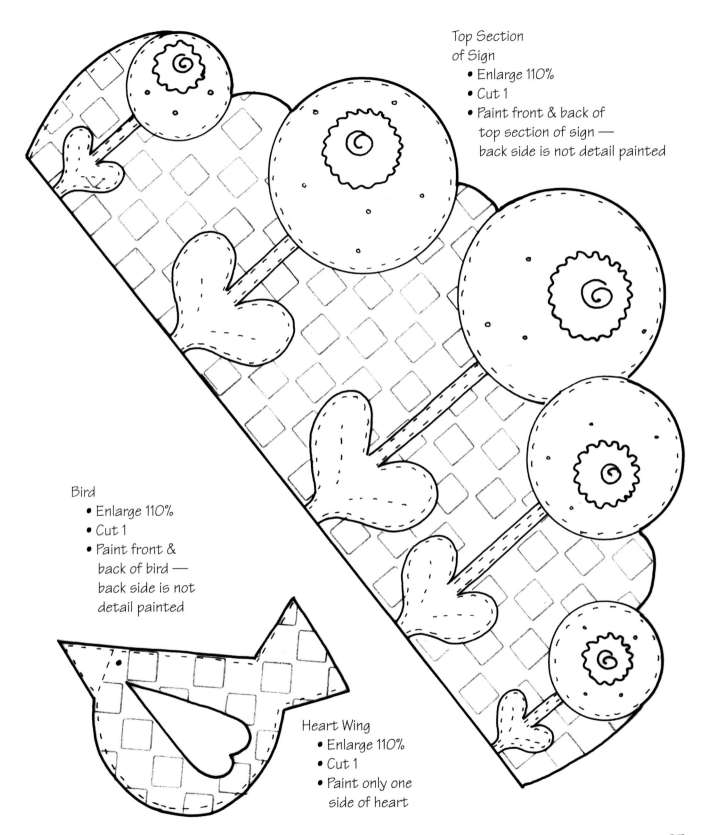

Top Section
of Sign
- Enlarge 110%
- Cut 1
- Paint front & back of
  top section of sign —
  back side is not detail painted

Bird
- Enlarge 110%
- Cut 1
- Paint front &
  back of bird —
  back side is not
  detail painted

Heart Wing
- Enlarge 110%
- Cut 1
- Paint only one
  side of heart

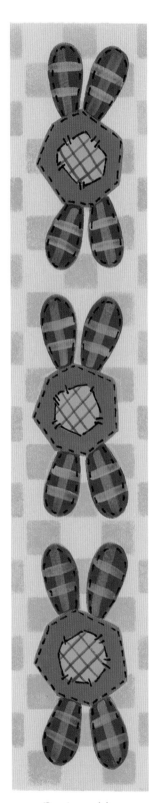

Birdhouse Welcome

Brushes:
Round fabric dye brush: #8
Flat brushes: #2, #10
Liner brush: #2
Old toothbrush

Acrylic Paint Colors:
Colonial blue, forest green, iron oxide, maple, midnight blue, spice, and white

Supplies:
Pine for birdhouse & sign:
　11" wide x 11" high x ³/₄" thick
Pine for bird:
　4" wide x 4" high x ¹/₄" thick
Stencil: ³/₈" checks
2-ply jute: (2) 16" pieces
Eye hooks: (4) ¹/₄"
Permanent black marker,
　fine-point
Wood glue
Antique spray stain, golden oak
Matte spray varnish
Drill with ¹/₁₆" drill bit

1. Transfer patterns, cut out shapes, and sand and seal wood for painting. Refer to General Instructions on page 6 for a list of supplies needed and for detailed information on preparing wood for painting.

2. Refer to General Instructions on pages 6-8 for detailed information on painting techniques that are used for this project.

3. Maple: Paint birdhouse, chimney, and sign on both sides.

4. Spice: Stencil ³/₈" checks on birdhouse and sign. Paint flower.

5. Colonial blue: Paint bird and top of chimney.

6. Midnight blue: Paint bird's wing.

7. Forest green: Paint leaves.

8. Spice: Apply dots on bird's wing and float-shade chimney and sign.

9. Iron oxide: Paint birdhouse's roof and foundation. Paint outside edge of sign. Paint flower's center. Paint lettering using a #2 flat brush. Spatter birdhouse and sign.

10. Midnight blue: Paint plaid lines in flower's center using a #2 liner brush. Apply dot for bird's eye.

11. Forest green: Mix with a little white. Stroke plaid on leaves using a #2 flat brush.

12. Line stitches and details on birdhouse, chimney, bird, flower, leaves, and sign with fine-point permanent black marker.

13. Finish with matte spray varnish because of linework.

14. Spray outer edges with antique spray stain.

15. Spray with matte spray varnish again.

16. Using wood glue, glue bird to birdhouse.

**Designed by
Kathy
Distefano Griffiths**

17. Drill $^{1}/_{16}$" holes into the bottom of the sign under the first and last letters of the word "Welcome." Drill one $^{1}/_{16}$" hole on each side in the roof of the birdhouse.

18. Screw eye hooks into drilled holes in sign and in birdhouse.

19. Thread 2-ply jute through left eye hook on birdhouse and through left eye hook on sign. Tie a knot to form a loop. Repeat on right side. Make sure to keep sides even. Cut off excess jute.

Welcome Sign
- Enlarge 130%
- Cut 1
- Paint front & back of welcome sign — back side is not detail painted

Birdhouse & Bird
- Enlarge 130%
- Cut 1 Birdhouse
- Cut 1 Bird
- Paint front & back of birdhouse — back side is not detail painted
- Paint only one side of bird

Birdhouse with Dormers

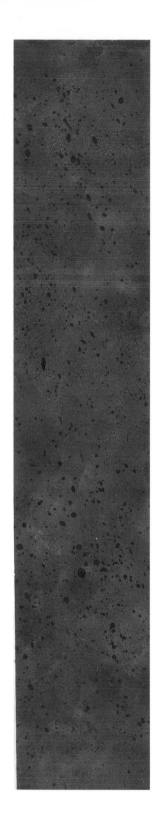

Birdhouse with Dormers

Brushes:
Round fabric dye brush: #8
Flat brushes: #2, #12
Liner brush: #00
Old toothbrush

Acrylic Paint Colors:
Antique white, burgundy, charcoal grey, evergreen, and rust

Supplies:
Pine for birdhouse:
Front,
    $5^1/4$" wide x 5" high x $^3/8$" thick
Back,
    $5^1/4$" wide x 5" high x $^3/8$" thick
Sides, (2)
    $3^1/8$" wide x $6^1/2$" high x $^3/8$" thick
Base,
    $6^1/4$" wide x 6" high x $^1/4$" thick
Roof, (2)
    $6^1/4$" wide x $3^1/2$" high x $^5/16$" thick
Porch roof,
    $5^1/4$" wide x $1^1/2$" high x $^3/8$" thick
Chimney,
    $^3/4$" wide x $1^1/2$" high x $^3/4$" thick
Door,
    $1^1/2$" wide x $1^1/8$" high x $^1/8$" thick
Windows, (2)
    1" wide x $1^1/4$" high x $^1/8$" thick
Dormers, (2)
    $^3/4$" wide x $1^1/2$" high x $1^1/2$" thick
Dormer roofs,
    (1) $^3/4$" wide x 2" high x $^1/8$" thick
    (1) $^7/8$" wide x 2" high x $^1/8$" thick
Wooden dowels in dormers:
    (2) $^1/8$" diameter x $^3/8$" length
Wooden dowel above door:
    (1) $^1/4$" diameter x 1" length
Wooden dowels for porch pillars:
    (2) $^3/8$" diameter x $3^1/2$" length

Spanish moss
Craft glue
Wood glue
Antique spray stain, golden oak
Matte spray varnish
Drill with $^1/8$", $^3/8$",
   $^1/4$" & $^3/4$" drill bits

1. Transfer patterns, cut out shapes, and sand and seal wood for painting. Refer to General Instructions on page 6 for a list of supplies needed and for detailed information on preparing wood for painting.

2. Drill one $^1/8$" hole in each dormer and drill one $^1/4$" hole above door to accommodate wooden dowels for perches. Drill two $^3/8$" holes in bottom side of porch roof and drill two $^3/8$" holes in top side of base to accommodate porch pillars (dowels). Drill $^1/4$" holes in dormers above holes for perches for openings in birdhouses. Drill one $^3/4$" hole in front of bird-house above hole for perch for opening in birdhouse.

3. Using wood glue, assemble birdhouse as shown in diagrams on page 103. Allow glue to dry thoroughly.

4. Refer to General Instructions on pages 6-8 for detailed information on painting tech-niques that are used for this project.

**Designed by
Debbie
Crabtree Lewis**

5. Evergreen: Paint base, roof, porch roof, and dormer roofs.

6. Burgundy: Paint birdhouse and dormers, including perches and openings in dormers.

7. Charcoal grey: Paint windows.

8. Antique white: Paint door, porch pillars, and perch above door. Line window frames using a #2 flat brush.

9. Evergreen: Mix with a little antique white. Stipple swags over windows and above drilled hole in front of birdhouse.

10. Antique white: Line ribbons on swags using a #00 liner brush.

11. Charcoal grey: Apply a dot for door handle. Spatter birdhouse and paint top of chimney.

12. Rust: Paint chimney.

13. Rust: Mix with a little antique white. Paint chimney bricks using a #2 flat brush.

14. Sand edges of birdhouse until unpainted wood is showing through.

15. Finish with matte spray varnish.

16. Lightly spray with antique spray stain.

17. Using craft glue, glue Spanish moss in opening in front of birdhouse.

Chimney
- Reproduce at 100%
- Paint brick pattern on all four sides of chimney

Swag
- Reproduce at 100%
- Paint pattern over windows & above drilled hole in front of birdhouse

Birdhouse Diagrams

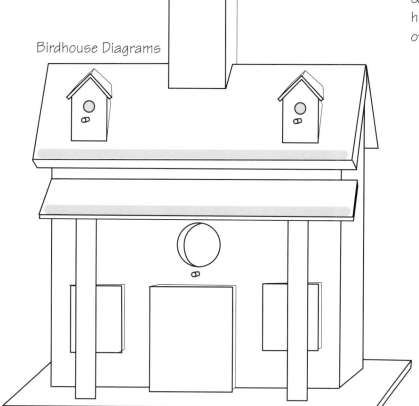

Front View of Birdhouse

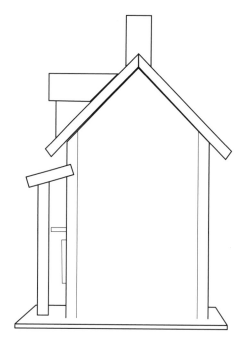

Side View of Birdhouse

3-Hole Birdhouse & Cat

Brushes:
Round fabric dye brush: #2
Flat brushes: #2, #4, #6, #8,
    #10, #12, #14, #16
Liner brush: #1
Old toothbrush

Acrylic Paint Colors:
Blush, colonial blue, colonial green, honey brown, medium green, wine, and yellow ochre

Supplies:
Pine for birdhouse:
    Front,
        3" wide x 15" high x 1/2" thick
    Back,
        3" wide x 15" high x 1/2" thick
    Sides, (2)
        1 1/2" wide x 11 3/4" high x 1/2" thick
    Base,
        4" wide x 4" high x 1/2" thick
Plywood for cat's body:
    4" wide x 5" high x 1/8" thick
Metal: 4" wide x 9 1/4" length
Wooden dowels:
    (3) 3/8" diameter x 1" length
Permanent black marker,
    fine-point
Wood glue
Matte spray varnish
Hammer
Nails: (4) 3/4"
Drill with 3/8" & 1" drill bits

1. Transfer patterns, cut out shapes, and sand and seal wood for painting. Refer to General Instructions on page 6 for a list of supplies needed and for detailed information on preparing wood for painting. Roof pitch is angled beginning at 17 3/4" height.

2. Drill three 3/8" holes in front of birdhouse to accommodate wooden dowels for perches. Drill three 1" holes down center front, evenly spaced and above holes for perches, for openings in birdhouse.

3. Using wood glue, assemble birdhouse as shown in diagram on page 106. Allow glue to dry thoroughly. For roof, bend metal in half and nail to birdhouse in two places on each side.

4. Refer to General Instructions on pages 6-8 for detailed information on painting techniques that are used for this project.

5. Colonial green: Paint birdhouse.

6. Colonial blue: Paint outside edge of base and paint wooden dowels for perches. Lightly spatter birdhouse.

7. Yellow ochre: Paint cat on both sides.

8. Blush: Apply blush to cat's cheeks using a #2 round fabric dye brush. Paint cat's nose.

**Designed by
Kathy
Distefano Griffiths**

9. Honey brown: Float-shade under cat's chin and around cat's leg. Wiggle all stripes on cat using a #1 liner brush.

10. Wine: Paint all wine-colored flowers on birdhouse and around cat's neck as shown in photograph on page 104 and on pattern on page 107.

11. Colonial blue: Paint all blue-colored flowers on birdhouse and around cat's neck as shown in photograph and on pattern.

12. Honey brown: Paint all honey-colored flowers on birdhouse and around cat's neck as shown in photograph and on pattern.

13. Medium green: Line flower stems using a #1 liner brush. Stroke leaves using a #2 flat brush.

14. Yellow ochre: Float-shade a half circle in the center of each flower.

15. Honey brown: Float-shade a smaller half circle on top of the yellow ochre centers on the wine- and blue-colored flowers.

16. Colonial blue: Float-shade a smaller half circle on top of the yellow ochre centers on the honey-colored flowers.

17. Line cat's face and line stitches on cat and flowers with fine-point permanent black marker.

18. Finish with matte spray varnish because of linework.

19. Using wood glue, glue cat to birdhouse as shown in photograph.

20. Spray with matte spray varnish again.

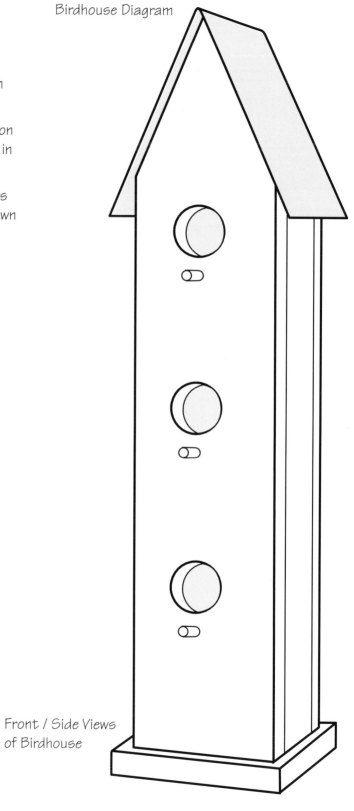

Birdhouse Diagram

Front / Side Views of Birdhouse

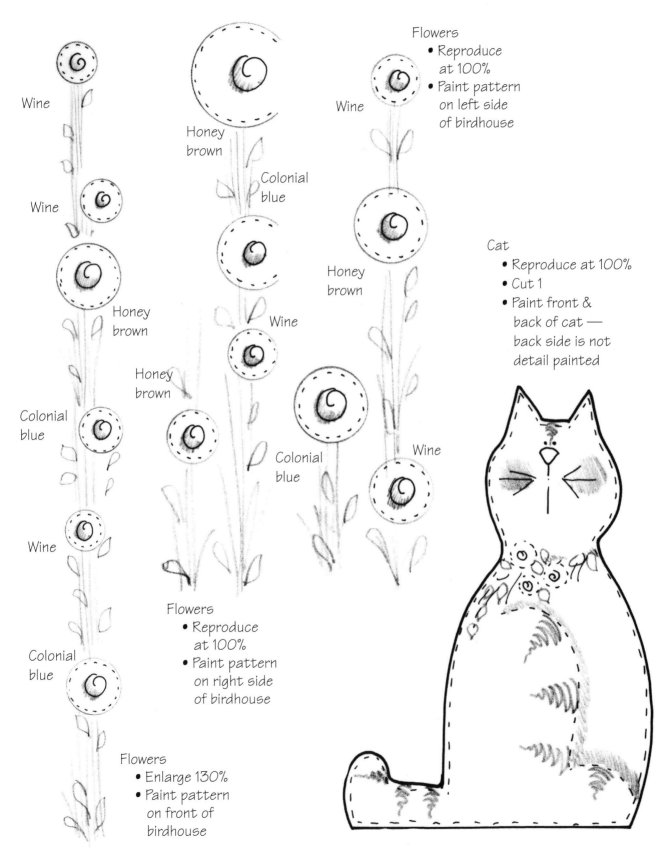

Wine

Wine

Honey
brown

Colonial
blue

Wine

Colonial
blue

Flowers
• Enlarge 130%
• Paint pattern
  on front of
  birdhouse

Honey
brown

Colonial
blue

Honey
brown

Wine

Colonial
blue

Flowers
• Reproduce
  at 100%
• Paint pattern
  on right side
  of birdhouse

Flowers
• Reproduce
  at 100%
• Paint pattern
  on left side
  of birdhouse

Wine

Honey
brown

Wine

Cat
• Reproduce at 100%
• Cut 1
• Paint front &
  back of cat —
  back side is not
  detail painted

Birdhouse For Rent

Brushes:
Round fabric dye brush: #8
Flat brushes: #6, #8, #20
Liner brush: #6/0
Old toothbrush

Acrylic Paint Colors:
Antique gold, antique white, black, blue-grey, bright yellow, burnt umber, khaki tan, midnight blue, tan, and true ochre

Supplies:
Pine for birdhouse:
  Front,
    $4^7/_8$" wide x 23" high x $^3/_4$" thick
  Back,
    $4^7/_8$" wide x 23" high x $^3/_4$" thick
  Sides, (2)
    4" wide x $17^1/_2$" high x $^3/_4$" thick
  Base,
    $6^3/_4$" wide x $7^1/_2$" high x $^3/_4$" thick
Pine for moon:
  $3^1/_2$" wide x $6^1/_2$" high x $^1/_4$" thick
Pine for sign:
  $1^1/_2$" wide x 7" high x $^1/_4$" thick
Pine for stars:
  $17^1/_2$" wide x 2" high x $^1/_4$" thick
Pine for bird:
  $3^1/_2$" wide x $1^1/_2$" high x $^1/_2$" thick
Chalkboards: (2) $9^1/_2$" wide x $7^1/_2$" high
19-gauge wire: (1) 8" piece
Stencils: $^3/_8$" checks &
  small stars & large stars
Linen jute: (1) 18" piece
2-ply jute: (2) 18" pieces
Grapevine wreath: (1) 6" diameter
Permanent black marker,
  fine-point

Industrial-strength glue
Wood glue
Antiquing medium
Clean cloth
Antique spray stain, golden oak
Matte spray varnish
Hammer
Nails: (3) Large, (4) Small
Drill with $^1/_8$" & $1^1/_4$" drill bits

1. Transfer patterns, cut out shapes, and sand and seal wood for painting. Refer to General Instructions on page 6 for a list of supplies needed and for detailed information on preparing wood for painting. Roof pitch is angled beginning at $11^3/_4$" height.

2. Using wood glue, assemble birdhouse as shown in diagram on page 111. Allow glue to dry thoroughly.

3. Drill two $^1/_8$" holes at top of the $7^1/_2$" sides of each chalkboard, 1" from each side. Drill three $1^1/_4$" holes down center front, evenly spaced, for openings in birdhouse. Drill one $^1/_8$" hole in bottom of bird. Drill one $^1/_8$" hole through the point of one star.

4. Refer to General Instructions on pages 6-8 for detailed information on painting techniques that are used for this project.

**Designed by
Jill
Webster**

5. Stain by applying antiquing medium to bird-house. Wipe off excess with a clean cloth. Repeat the process for a richer, darker color.

6. Blue-grey: Wash bird.

7. Burnt umber: Spatter bird. Lightly dry-brush bird's tail feathers.

8. Sand edges of bird until unpainted wood is showing through.

9. Black: Apply dots for bird's eyes and paint bird's beak.

10. Antique white: Paint sign.

11. Khaki tan: Stencil $3/8$" checks on front of sign.

12. Tan: Float-shade edges of sign and very lightly float-shade left side of each check.

13. Black: Paint lettering on sign.

14. Line details on sign with fine-point permanent black marker.

15. Burnt umber: Spatter sign.

16. Bright yellow: Paint moon and all stars.

17. True ochre: Float-shade edges of moon and stars and paint lines on stars.

18. Antique gold: Paint lines on moon.

19. Line details on moon and stars with fine-point permanent black marker.

20. Burnt umber: Spatter moon and stars.

21. Antique white: Paint chalkboard centers.

22. Midnight blue: Paint base and chalkboard frames.

23. Khaki tan: Randomly stencil small and large stars on chalkboard centers.

24. Tan: Float-shade along inside edges of chalk-boards.

25. Antique white: Spatter chalkboards.

26. Khaki tan: Spatter chalkboards.

27. Tan: Spatter chalkboards.

28. Burnt umber: Spatter base and lightly spatter birdhouse.

29. Hammer large nails into birdhouse for perches $5/8$" below $1 1/4$" hole openings.

30. Using small nails, nail moon above top hole opening. Nail sign between top two hole openings. Nail two stars to front edge of one chalkboard.

31. Using wood glue, glue two stars to each chalkboard center.

32. Thread 2-ply jute through drilled holes in tops of both chalkboards and tie them together so the tops are touching. Place chalkboards at top of birdhouse to form a roof.

33. Using industrial-strength glue, glue one end of 8" piece of 19-gauge wire into hole in bottom of bird. Tightly wrap wire around center "nail perch" until bird sits nicely.

34. Thread linen jute through hole in point of star and tie a knot, leaving one long tail. Glue end of long tail to bird's beak so it hangs.

35. Unravel grapevine wreath and wrap it around birdhouse.

36. Spray chalkboard roof around outer edges with antique spray stain.

37. Spray with matte spray varnish.

Star
- Reproduce at 100%
- Cut 7
- Paint fronts & backs of stars

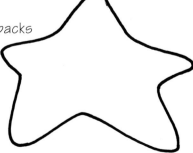

110

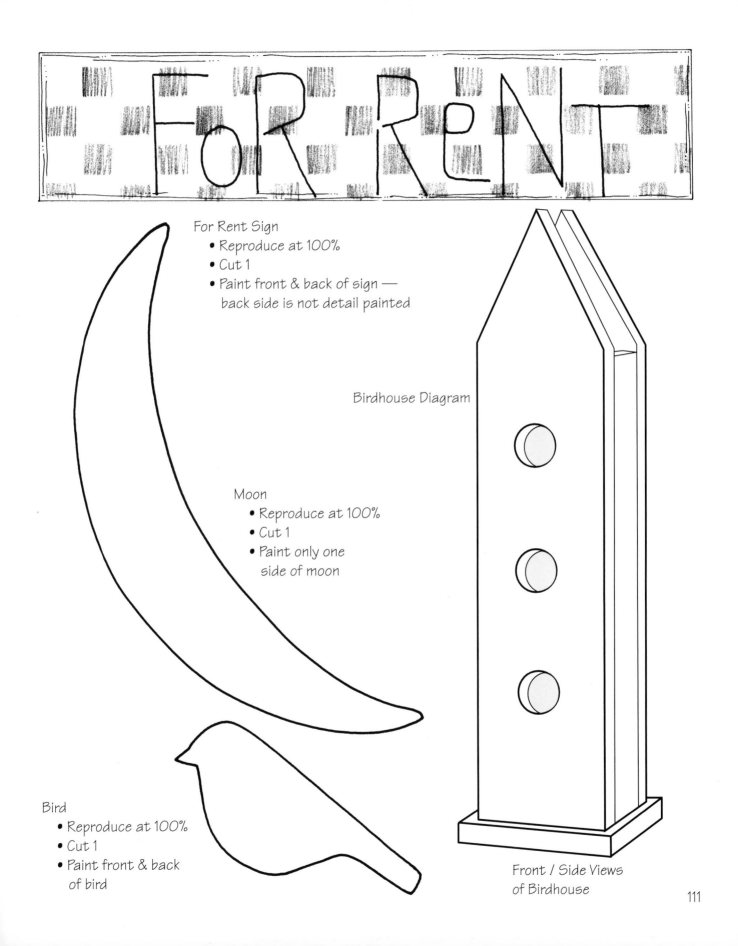

For Rent Sign
- Reproduce at 100%
- Cut 1
- Paint front & back of sign — back side is not detail painted

Birdhouse Diagram

Moon
- Reproduce at 100%
- Cut 1
- Paint only one side of moon

Bird
- Reproduce at 100%
- Cut 1
- Paint front & back of bird

Front / Side Views of Birdhouse

Pine Shingles Birdhouse

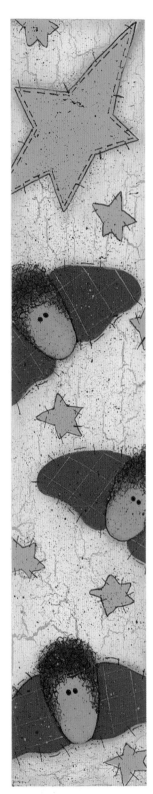

**Designed by
Jill
Webster**

Brushes:
Flat brushes: #6, #8, #20
Liner brush: #6/0

Acrylic Paint Colors:
Antique gold, antique maroon,
antique white, black, Caucasian flesh,
clay, dark colonial blue, khaki tan,
midnight blue, raw sienna, rust,
and yellow ochre

Supplies:
Pine for birdhouse:
  Front,
    6" wide x 7" high x $^3/_4$" thick
  Back,
    6" wide x 7" high x $^3/_4$" thick
  Sides, (2)
    2" wide x 4$^1/_2$" high x $^3/_4$" thick
  Base,
    6" wide x 7" high x $^1/_2$" thick
  Roof (Shingles), (6)
    1$^3/_4$" wide x 6" high x $^1/_4$" thick
  Door,
    2" wide x 4$^1/_4$" high x $^1/_4$" thick
Pine for angel wings:
  4$^1/_2$" wide x 2" high x $^1/_4$" thick
Pine for bird:
  2$^1/_4$" wide x 1$^1/_4$" high x $^1/_4$" thick
Pine for small birdhouse:
  1$^1/_2$" wide x 1$^1/_2$" high x $^3/_4$" thick
Pine for large star:
  5" wide x 3$^1/_2$" high x $^3/_8$" thick
Plywood for small stars:
  6" wide x 2" high x $^1/_4$" thick
Wooden dowels:
  (1) $^1/_4$" diameter x 2" length
  (1) $^1/_8$" diameter x $^3/_4$" length
Wooden flower pot: (1) 1$^1/_2$"
Wooden half egg: (1) 1"

19-gauge wire:
  (1) 3" piece
  (1) 6" piece
Linen jute: (1) 9" piece
Eye hooks: (2) $^1/_4$"
Raffia
Floral foam
Dried flowers
Craft glue
Industrial-strength glue
Wood glue
Antiquing medium
Clean cloth
Weathered wood crackling medium
Antique spray stain, golden oak
Needlenose pliers
Drill with $^1/_{16}$", $^1/_8$", $^1/_4$" & 1" drill bits

1. Transfer patterns, cut out shapes, and sand and seal wood for painting. Refer to General Instructions on page 6 for a list of supplies needed and for detailed information on preparing wood for painting.

2. Using wood glue, assemble birdhouse as shown in diagram on page 115. Allow glue to dry thoroughly.

3. Drill one 1" hole through door for opening in birdhouse. Drill one $^1/_4$" hole in door to accommodate wooden dowel for perch. Drill one $^1/_{16}$" hole in top center of birdhouse roof and one $^1/_{16}$" hole in bottom of star. Drill two $^1/_8$" holes similar to those in a button through the center of star. Drill one $^1/_{16}$" hole in right

side of small birdhouse's roof and one $1/16$" hole in top center of small birdhouse. Drill one $1/8$" hole in small birdhouse to accommodate wooden dowel for perch. Drill one $1/4$" hole in small birdhouse for opening in birdhouse. Drill one $1/16$" hole in bottom of bird.

4. Refer to General Instructions on pages 6-8 for detailed information on painting techniques that are used for this project.

5. Khaki tan: Paint birdhouse and small birdhouse.

6. Antique maroon: Paint base, door, and inside hole in door.

7. Midnight blue: Paint roof on both sides.

8. Paint birdhouse, including roof, and base with weathered wood crackling medium. Allow crackling medium to dry for approximately 15 to 20 minutes.

9. Dark colonial blue: Paint angel's wings.

10. Black: Paint bird on both sides.

11. Clay: Paint wooden flower pot.

12. Rust: Paint small birdhouse's roof. Paint wooden dowels.

13. Antique maroon: Lightly dry-brush wooden flower pot.

14. Clay: Lightly dry-brush over antique maroon on wooden flower pot.

15. Yellow ochre: Paint bird's beak.

16. Antique gold: Paint all stars.

17. Midnight blue: Paint plaid lines down and across angel's wings.

18. Antique gold: Paint thin lines down and across angel's wings between midnight blue lines.

19. Caucasian flesh: Paint wooden half egg for angel's face.

20. Raw sienna: Stipple hair on angel's head.

21. Rust: Stipple hair.

22. Black: Apply dots for angel's eyes. Line details in angel's hair using a #6/0 liner brush.

23. Sand edges of stars and angel's wings.

24. Antique white: Paint over crackling medium on birdhouse, except on door, and roof.

25. Antique maroon: Paint over crackling medium on base and door.

26. Midnight blue: Paint edges and top of roof.

27. Antique by applying antiquing medium to all wood pieces. Wipe off excess with a clean cloth.

28. Using wood glue, glue small stars to birdhouse's roof. Glue angel's face to angel's wings and glue angel above door. Glue wooden dowels for perches inside drilled hole in door and inside drilled hole in small birdhouse. Glue wooden flower pot to front corner of base.

29. Using industrial-strength glue, glue one end of 6" piece of 19-gauge wire into hole in bottom of bird. Tightly wrap wire around perch until bird sits nicely. Glue one end of 3" piece of 19-gauge wire into hole in top center of birdhouse. Twist and curl wire and glue the other end into hole in bottom of star.

30. Thread linen jute through holes in center of star and tie in a bow.

31. Screw eye hooks into drilled holes in top of small birdhouse and in right side of roof. Using needlenose pliers, open up "eye" in hook attached to small birdhouse to make a hook. Hook it through the eye hook on roof.

32. Using craft glue, glue floral foam into wooden flower pot. Glue dried flowers into flower pot.

33. Tie a raffia bow and glue it under angel's face on angel's wings.

34. Spray birdhouse with antique spray stain, spraying the edges a little heavier.

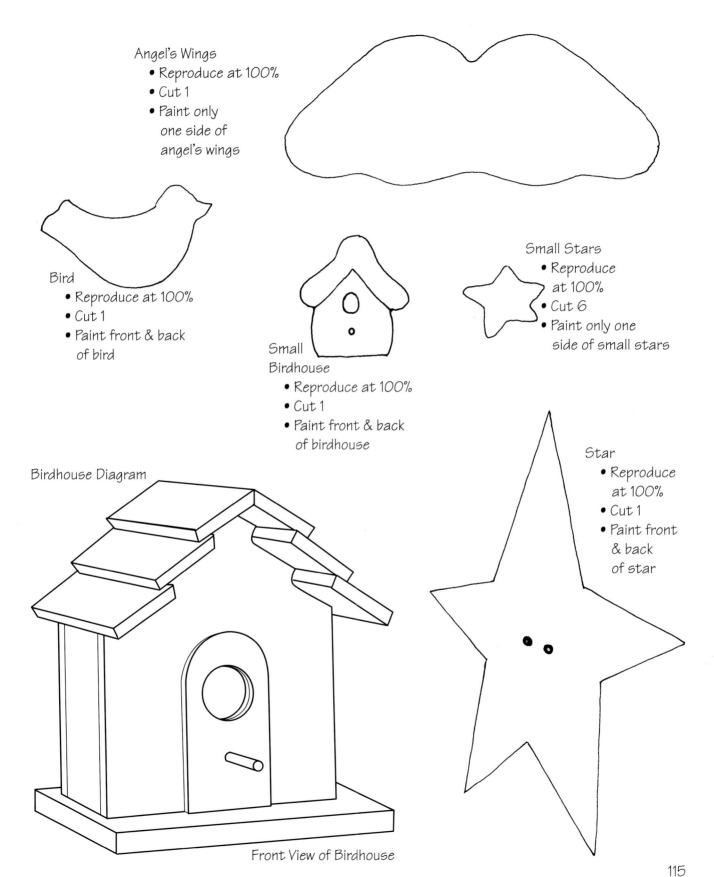

Angel's Wings
- Reproduce at 100%
- Cut 1
- Paint only one side of angel's wings

Bird
- Reproduce at 100%
- Cut 1
- Paint front & back of bird

Small Birdhouse
- Reproduce at 100%
- Cut 1
- Paint front & back of birdhouse

Small Stars
- Reproduce at 100%
- Cut 6
- Paint only one side of small stars

Star
- Reproduce at 100%
- Cut 1
- Paint front & back of star

Birdhouse Diagram

Front View of Birdhouse

Pine Shingles Birdhouse
Front & Back Pattern
- Reproduce at 100%
- Cut 2 —
    1 for front &
    1 for back

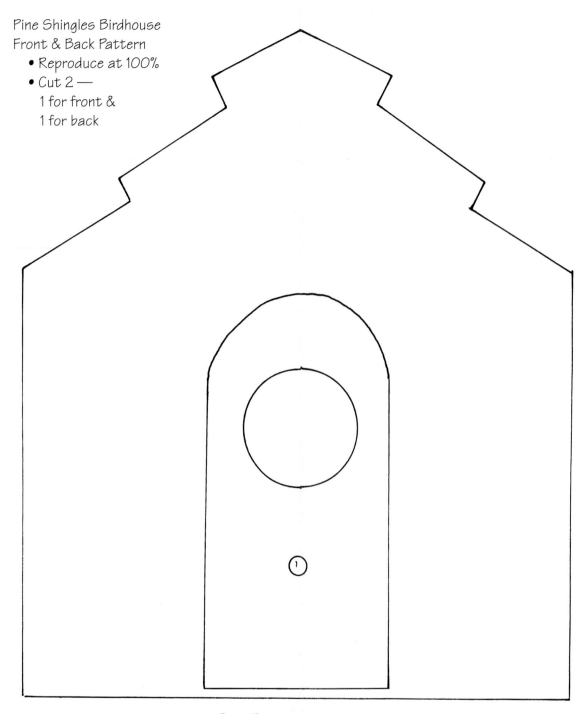

Door Pattern
- Reproduce at 100%
- Cut 1

Rosebud Birdhouse

Rosebud Birdhouse

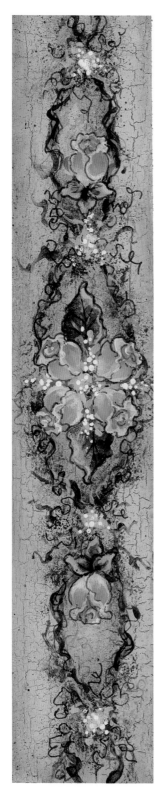

**Designed by
Emily
Dinsdale**

Brushes:
Flat brushes: #2, #8
Old toothbrush

Acrylic Paint Colors:
Brown-grey, dark chocolate, dark green, parchment, and rose beige

Supplies:
Pine for birdhouse:
    $3^1/2$" wide x 5" high x 2" thick
Pine for roof:
    (1) 3" wide x 2" high x $1/4$" thick
    (1) $3^1/4$" wide x 2" high x $1/4$" thick
Pine for bird's body:
    2" wide x 2" high x $1/2$" thick
Pine for bird's wings:
    $1^1/4$" wide x $1^1/2$" high x $1/4$" thick
Wooden dowels:
    (1) $1/8$" diameter x $1^1/2$" length
    (1) $1/8$" diameter x $3/4$" length
19-gauge wire: (1) 15" piece
Raffia
Dried moss, green
Dried rosebuds
Craft glue
Industrial-strength glue
Wood glue
Antique spray stain, golden oak
Matte spray varnish
Needlenose pliers
Drill with $1/16$", $1/8$" & $7/8$" drill bits

1.   Transfer patterns, cut out shapes, and sand and seal wood for painting. Refer to General Instructions on page 6 for a list of supplies needed and for detailed information on preparing wood for painting.

2.   Drill one $1/8$" hole in birdhouse to accommodate wooden dowel for perch. Drill one $7/8$" hole in birdhouse, $1/2$ of the way through, for opening in birdhouse. Drill one $1/16$" hole in right side of roof and one $1/16$" hole in left side of roof. Drill one $1/8$" hole in top center of birdhouse roof and one $1/8$" hole in bottom of bird.

3.   Using wood glue, glue birdhouse's roof to birdhouse as shown in diagram on page 119. Allow glue to dry thoroughly.

4.   Refer to General Instructions on pages 6-8 for detailed information on painting techniques that are used for this project.

5.   Rose beige: Paint birdhouse on both sides. Paint wooden dowels.

6.   Dark green: Paint roof on both sides.

7.   Brown-grey: Paint bird's body and bird's wings on both sides.

8.   Parchment: Paint bird's beak on both sides.

9.   Dark chocolate: Paint inside drilled hole for opening in birdhouse. Apply dots for bird's eyes. Lightly spatter bird and birdhouse on both sides.

10.   Sand edges of bird and birdhouse until unpainted wood is showing through.

11. Carefully spray the drilled hole for opening in birdhouse, outer edges of birdhouse, and bird on both sides with antique spray stain.

12. Using wood glue, glue bird's wings on bird. Glue wooden dowel for perch inside drilled hole in birdhouse. Glue wooden dowel inside drilled holes in bottom of bird and top of birdhouse.

13. Curl the 19-gauge wire and, using industrial-strength glue, glue one end of wire into hole on right side of birdhouse's roof. Glue the other end into hole on left side of birdhouse's roof.

14. Tie raffia bows around 19-gauge wire as shown in photograph on page 117.

15. Using craft glue, glue dried moss and rose-buds to birdhouse as shown in photograph.

16. Finish with matte spray varnish.

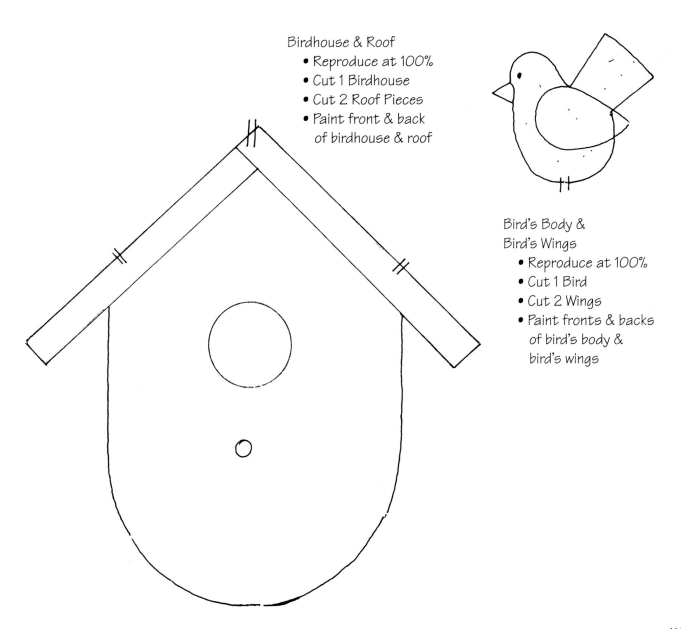

Birdhouse & Roof
- Reproduce at 100%
- Cut 1 Birdhouse
- Cut 2 Roof Pieces
- Paint front & back of birdhouse & roof

Bird's Body & Bird's Wings
- Reproduce at 100%
- Cut 1 Bird
- Cut 2 Wings
- Paint fronts & backs of bird's body & bird's wings

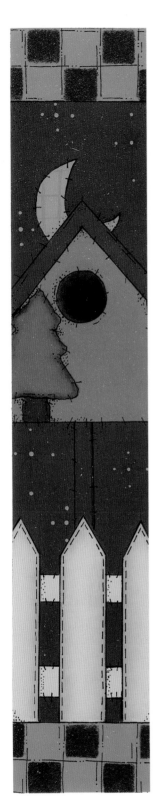

**Designed by
Jill
Webster**

Birdhouse Planter Box

Brushes:
Round fabric dye brush: #14
Flat brush: #8
Liner brush: #6/0
Old toothbrush

Acrylic Paint Colors:
Antique white, blue-grey, dark chocolate, dark green, maroon, medium green, mink, and true ochre

Supplies:
Cedar for planter box:
   Front,
      $10^3/4$" wide x 4" high x $3/4$" thick
   Back,
      $10^3/4$" wide x 4" high x $3/4$" thick
   Sides, (2)
      $4^1/2$" wide x 3" high x $3/4$" thick
   Bottom, $10^3/4$" wide x
      $4^1/2$" high x $3/4$" thick
   Top edges,
      (2) 12" wide x $1^1/2$" high x
         $3/4$" thick with 45° corner
      (2) $7^1/2$" wide x $1^1/2$" high x
         $3/4$" thick with 45° corner
Pine for birdhouse:
   4" wide x 5" high x $1^1/2$" thick
Pine for birdhouse's roof:
   $5^3/4$" wide x 2" high x $1/4$" thick
Pine for pickets:
   9" wide x 6" high x $1/4$" thick
Pine for fence side rails:
   10" wide x 3" high x $1/4$" thick
Plywood for tree, moon & sign:
   7" wide x $3^1/2$" high x $1/8$" thick
Wooden dowel:
   (1) $3/8$" diameter x 12" length
Stencils: $1/4$" checks & $1/2$" checks
Linen jute: (1) 6" piece
Permanent black marker,
   fine-point

Wood glue
Antique spray stain, golden oak
Matte spray varnish
Hammer
Nail: (1) $3/4$"
Drill with $1/16$", $3/8$" & 1" drill bits

1. Transfer patterns, cut out shapes, and sand and seal wood for painting. Refer to General Instructions on page 6 for a list of supplies needed and for detailed information on preparing wood for painting. The cedar for the planter box need not be sealed with wood sealer.

2. Drill one 1" hole in front of birdhouse, $2/3$ of the way through, for opening in birdhouse. Drill one $3/8$" hole in bottom center of birdhouse. Drill one $1/16$" hole in each corner at top of sign.

3. Using wood glue, assemble planter box as shown in diagrams on page 122 and glue roof on birdhouse as shown on pattern on page 123. Assemble picket fence, making sure the bottoms of all "pickets" are even. Allow glue to dry thoroughly. If desired, secure planter box with nails.

4. Drill one $3/8$" hole in top edge of back of planter box 3" from left edge. Drill two $3/8$" holes through bottom of planter box for drainage.

5. Refer to General Instructions on pages 6-8 for detailed information on painting techniques that are used for this project.

6. Dark green: Stencil three rows of ½" checks around the bottom front of planter box.

7. Lightly spray planter box with antique spray stain.

8. Antique white: Paint picket fence.

9. Mink: Float-shade edges around picket fence.

10. Blue-grey: Paint birdhouse.

11. Antique white: Spatter birdhouse.

12. Maroon: Paint birdhouse's roof.

13. Dark green: Stencil ¼" checks on front edge of roof. Paint tree on both sides and paint wooden dowel.

14. Dark chocolate: Paint tree trunk.

15. True ochre: Paint moon and sign.

16. Antique white: Stencil ¼" checks on front of sign.

17. Medium green: Paint stripe around sign using a #6/0 liner brush.

18. Line stitches around outside edges of picket fence with fine-point permanent black marker. Line around birdhouse and sign. Line lettering on sign.

19. Finish with matte spray varnish because of linework.

20. Using wood glue, glue wooden dowel inside hole in top of planter box. Glue top end of wooden dowel inside hole in bottom of birdhouse. Glue tree and moon to front of birdhouse as shown in photograph on page 120. Glue picket fence to top inside edge of back of planter box in front of wooden dowel. Allow glue to dry thoroughly.

21. Hammer the nail for perch into center front of birdhouse near the bottom.

22. Thread linen jute through holes in sign and tie a knot to form a loop for hanging. Hang sign from nail perch.

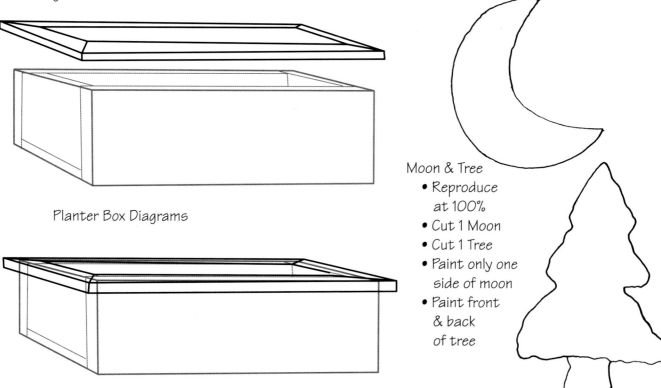

Planter Box Diagrams

Moon & Tree
• Reproduce at 100%
• Cut 1 Moon
• Cut 1 Tree
• Paint only one side of moon
• Paint front & back of tree

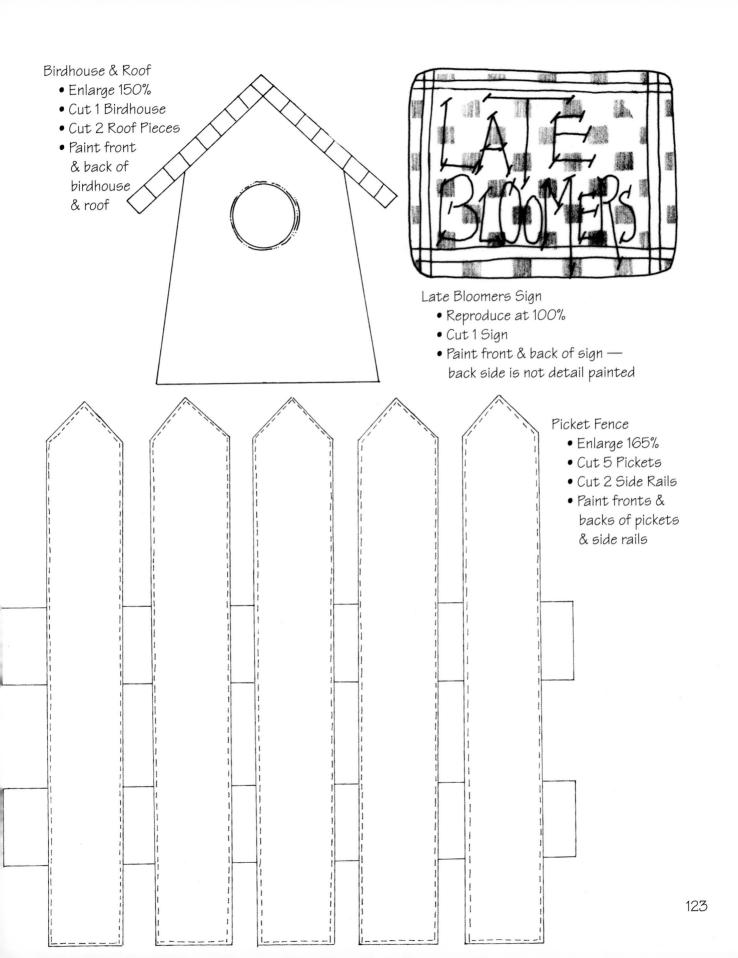

Birdhouse & Roof
- Enlarge 150%
- Cut 1 Birdhouse
- Cut 2 Roof Pieces
- Paint front
  & back of
  birdhouse
  & roof

Late Bloomers Sign
- Reproduce at 100%
- Cut 1 Sign
- Paint front & back of sign —
  back side is not detail painted

Picket Fence
- Enlarge 165%
- Cut 5 Pickets
- Cut 2 Side Rails
- Paint fronts &
  backs of pickets
  & side rails

123

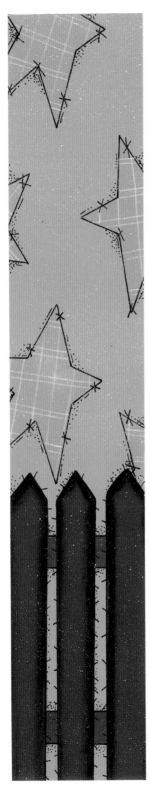

Picket Fence Planter

Brushes:
Flat brushes: #6, #8
Old toothbrush

Acrylic Paint Colors:
Antique white, black, burnt umber, medium green, midnight blue, and true ochre

Supplies:
Pine for pickets:
   6" wide x 15" high x ¼" thick
Pine for fence side rails:
   24" wide x 1½" high x ¼" thick
Plywood for tree & star:
   4" wide x 8" high x ⅛" thick
Linen jute: (8) 6" pieces
Wood glue
Matte spray varnish
Drill with ⅛" drill bit

1. Transfer patterns, cut out shapes, and sand and seal wood for painting. Refer to General Instructions on page 6 for a list of supplies needed and for detailed information on preparing wood for painting.

2. Drill one ⅛" hole in the center of each end in side rails.

3. Refer to General Instructions on pages 6-8 for detailed information on painting techniques that are used for this project.

4. Midnight blue: Paint pickets and side rails.

5. Black: Float-shade edges around pickets and side rails.

6. Sand edges of pickets until unpainted wood is showing through.

7. Antique white: Spatter pickets.

8. Using wood glue, glue each side of picket fence together. Each side will consist of two side rails and three pickets. Make sure side rails are glued evenly in the center back of pickets. Allow glue to dry thoroughly.

9. True ochre: Paint star.

10. Medium green: Paint tree.

11. Burnt umber: Paint tree trunk.

12. Sand edges of star and tree until unpainted wood is showing through.

13. Thread linen jute through drilled holes in side rails and tie each piece into a bow.

14. Using wood glue, glue star and tree to one side of picket fence as shown in photograph on page 124.

15. Finish with matte spray varnish.

**Designed by
Jill
Webster**

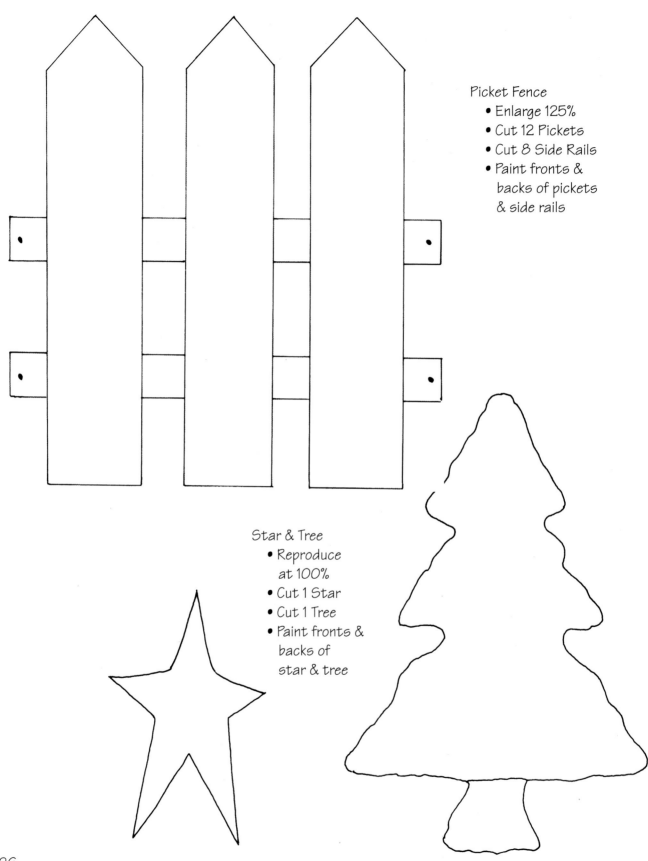

Picket Fence
- Enlarge 125%
- Cut 12 Pickets
- Cut 8 Side Rails
- Paint fronts & backs of pickets & side rails

Star & Tree
- Reproduce at 100%
- Cut 1 Star
- Cut 1 Tree
- Paint fronts & backs of star & tree

Metric Conversion Chart

INCHES TO MILLIMETRES AND CENTIMETRES

MM-Millimetres   CM-Centimetres

INCHES	MM	CM	INCHES	CM	INCHES	CM
1/8	3	0.9	9	22.9	30	76.2
1/4	6	0.6	10	25.4	31	78.7
3/8	10	1.0	11	27.9	32	81.3
1/2	13	1.3	12	30.5	33	83.8
5/8	16	1.6	13	33.0	34	86.4
3/4	19	1.9	14	35.6	35	88.9
7/8	22	2.2	15	38.1	36	91.4
1	25	2.5	16	40.6	37	94.0
1 1/4	32	3.2	17	43.2	38	96.5
1 1/2	38	3.8	18	45.7	39	99.1
1 3/4	44	4.4	19	48.3	40	101.6
2	51	5.1	20	50.8	41	104.1
2 1/2	64	6.4	21	53.3	42	106.7
3	76	7.6	22	55.9	43	109.2
3 1/2	89	8.9	23	58.4	44	111.8
4	102	10.2	24	61.0	45	114.3
4 1/2	114	11.4	25	63.5	46	116.8
5	127	12.7	26	66.0	47	119.4
6	152	15.2	27	68.6	48	121.9
7	178	17.8	28	71.1	49	124.5
8	203	20.3	29	73.7	50	127.0

YARDS TO METRES

YARDS	METRES	YARDS	METRES	YARDS	METRES	YARDS	METRES	YARDS	METRES
1/8	0.11	2 1/8	1.94	4 1/8	3.77	6 1/8	5.60	8 1/8	7.43
1/4	0.23	2 1/4	2.06	4 1/4	3.89	6 1/4	5.72	8 1/4	7.54
3/8	0.34	2 3/8	2.17	4 3/8	4.00	6 3/8	5.83	8 3/8	7.66
1/2	0.46	2 1/2	2.29	4 1/2	4.11	6 1/2	5.94	8 1/2	7.77
5/8	0.57	2 5/8	2.40	4 5/8	4.23	6 5/8	6.06	8 5/8	7.89
3/4	0.69	2 3/4	2.51	4 3/4	4.34	6 3/4	6.17	8 3/4	8.00
7/8	0.80	2 7/8	2.63	4 7/8	4.46	6 7/8	6.29	8 7/8	8.12
1	0.91	3	2.74	5	4.57	7	6.40	9	8.23
1 1/8	1.03	3 1/8	2.86	5 1/8	4.69	7 1/8	6.52	9 1/8	8.34
1 1/4	1.14	3 1/4	2.97	5 1/4	4.80	7 1/4	6.63	9 1/4	8.46
1 3/8	1.26	3 3/8	3.09	5 3/8	4.91	7 3/8	6.74	9 3/8	8.57
1 1/2	1.37	3 1/2	3.20	5 1/2	5.03	7 1/2	6.86	9 1/2	8.69
1 5/8	1.49	3 5/8	3.31	5 5/8	5.14	7 5/8	6.97	9 5/8	8.80
1 3/4	1.60	3 3/4	3.43	5 3/4	5.26	7 3/4	7.09	9 3/4	8.92
1 7/8	1.71	3 7/8	3.54	5 7/8	5.37	7 7/8	7.20	9 7/8	9.03
2	1.83	4	3.66	6	5.49	8	7.32	10	9.14

Index

Adding Dots 6
Antique Finishing 6-7
Antiquing 7
Ark Wind Chime 76-80
Assembling Windmills & Whirligigs 9
Barnyard Friends Chalkboard 45-47
Base Coating 7
Beehive Whirligig 52, 58, 61
Birdhouse For Rent 108-111
Birdhouse Planter Box 120-123
Birdhouse Welcome 98-100
Birdhouse with Dormers 101-103
Birdhouses 101-123
Bunny & Carrots Whirligig 70-72
Cat & Bird Windmill 55-57
Chalkboards 42-47
Cock-A-Doodle-Doo Chalkboard 42-44
Country Girl 28-31
Curling Wire 7
Dove Weathervane 87-89
Dry Brushing 7
Every Bunny Loves A Garden Wind Chime 81-83
Fat Cat Wind Chime 73-75
Float Shading 7
Garden Stakes 14-19
General Instructions 6-8
Guardian Bunny 24-27
Honey Bear Windmill 52-54
Ladybug Windmill 48-51
Linework 7
Metric Conversion Chart 127
Noah & Friends Whirligig 65-69
Old Mac's Farm 20-23
Painting 7
Picket Fence Planter 124-126
Pine Shingles Birdhouse 112-116
Plaid Chicken Boxes 10-13
Preparing Wood for Painting 6
Rabbit on Rooster Whirligig 62-64
Rooster Weathervane 84-86
Rosebud Birdhouse 117-119
S.S. Ark Weathervane 90-93
Sitting Rabbit Garden Stake 14-16
Sitting Rooster Garden Stake 17-19
Spattering 8
Stenciling 8
Stippling 8
Stroking 8
3-Hole Birdhouse & Cat 104-107
To The Garden Sign 94-97
Varnishing 8
Washing 8
Watering Can Whirligig 59-61
Weathervanes 84-93
Welcome Bee Keeper 32-41
Whirligigs 9, 52, 58-72
Wind Chimes 73-83
Windmills 9, 48-57

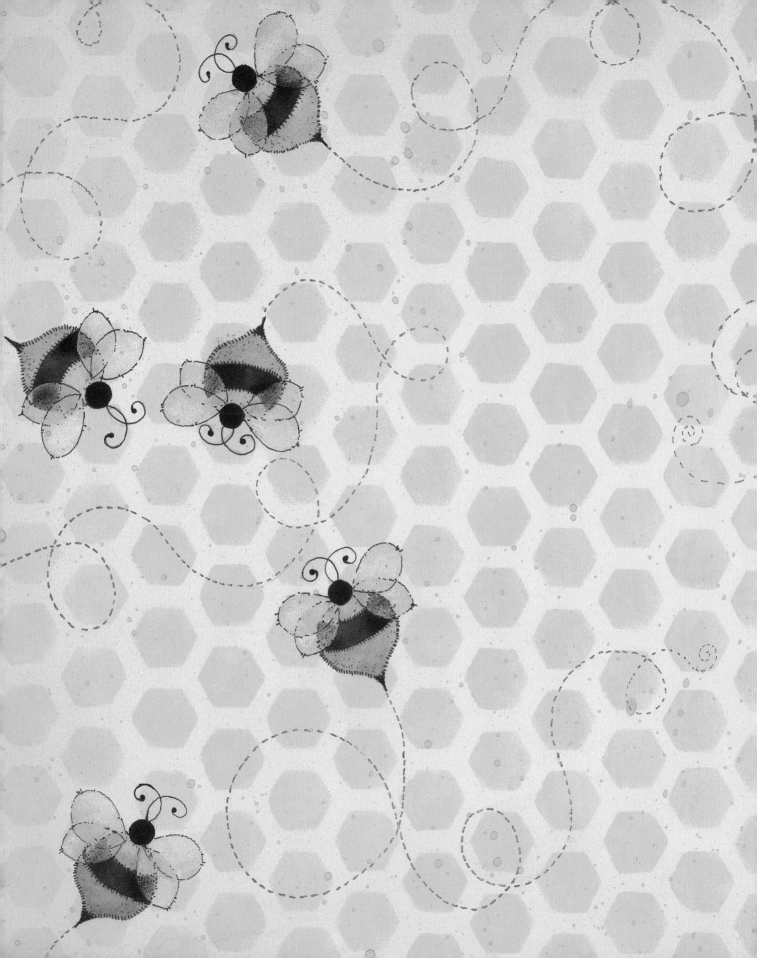